GRASSROOT DEMOCRACY IN INDIAN SOCIETY

About the Author

Ganapathy Palanithurai, Professor in Rajiv Gandhi Chair, Gandhigram Rural Institute is an academic activist working with the people in rural areas for building the capacity of the leaders and people to reinvent sustainable grass-root democracy. He is heading the department of Political Science and Development Administration in Gandhigram Rural University, Tamil Nadu. His policy advocacy role at the governmental level is increasingly felt at present in all the three levels namely sub-regional, regional and national as he does more field work than theorization. He has been associating himself with State Planning Commission of Tamil Nadu, Population Foundation of India, Rajiv Gandhi Foundation, CAPART, Ministry of Rural Areas and Employment in specific areas of activities in connection with empowerment of people. He is in the network of the Non-Governmental Organisations for panchayat activities. He involves himself in capacity building exercise for local body leaders for all political parties. He has evolved training module and manual for local body leaders. He has to his credit twenty-four books, seventy-five articles in reputed journals, ten working papers, seven monographs, seven review articles on three major areas namely, Legislative Behaviour, Ethnicity and Panchayati Raj System. He was a recipient of Fellowship from Sastri Indo-Canadian Institute, New Delhi and World Academy of Art and Science, USA. He has visited the US and Canada, on academic assignments. He is a life member of Indian Institute of Public Administration, Indian Association of Public Administration, Indian Association of Political Science, Indian Association of American Studies, and Indian Association of Canadian Studies.

GRASSROOT DEMOCRACY IN INDIAN SOCIETY

G. PALANITHURAI
Rajiv Gandhi Chair for Panchayati Raj Studies
Deptt. of Political Science and Development Administration
The Gandhigram Rural Institute Deemed University
Gandhigram (T.N.)

CONCEPT PUBLISHING COMPANY, NEW DELHI - 110059

ISBN 81-7022-808-5

First Published 2000

Published and Printed by
Ashok Kumar Mittal
Concept Publishing Company
A/15-16, Commercial Block, Mohan Garden,
NEW DELHI - 110059 (India)

Phones : 5648039, 5649024
Fax : 91-11-5598898

TO
THE DIVINE MOTHER

"To make a new India, we need not only industrial progress and political maturity. but a renewal of faith in the future of our country. . . . We cannot have national integration without national discipline and without a national ethos. Decency in public life should be maintained. We need the dedicated effort of all our citizens."

— Dr. S. Radhakrishnan

Preface

The essays included in this volume have been written during the past two years in response to invitations of various organisations to contribute to seminars and learned publications. The essays have been written for a specific purpose with a time stipulation. Writing any article or essay within a timeframe that too in Indian context has its own limitations. Perfection could not be achieved but that cannot be the excuse. But the timeframe has compelled the author many times to complete the assignments before the deadline. The write-up which has been prepared for a specific requirement has been circulated for a wider consumption. The reactions over the articles have been the source of strength for the author to rewrite the same. On most of the occasions the articles would not have been written, but for the pressure to meet the deadline.

The essays are on a variety of topics touching many vital aspects of governance that too in the rural society. Some practical demonstrations have also been done at the micro-level. Fairly a good deal of issues have been discussed in the essays of this volume which will stimulate the thinking of the common and committed citizens of the society in India. Though variegated issues have been raised and discussed, all of them have been brought into a specific focus: Grassroot Democracy In Indian Society. One would find the structural unity in all the essays. I took pains to correct the articles based on the comments of some of the participants of the seminars and it is more than writing a new one. It is painful to rewrite or correct the essays already written and yet I have done it so as to bring the issues for discussion at a higher level for wider audience. One may observe a few repetitions that could not and should not be removed as they would affect the cogence and coherence of the write-up. Further a few arguments and appeals would appear more than once with a specific purpose of underlining the underpinnings of the whole argument. It may read an activist posture of the issues as the author is a known committed academician working towards empowering people as an alternative to the existing malaised institutions of governance.

The author expresses his indebtedness to many as his success is always perceived as a success of a team which has got a commitment towards empowerment of the people. A band of committed workers in the name of teachers, research associates, research officers and volunteers in some non-governmental organisations has joined together to help the author not only in writing articles and papers but mostly in conducting novel experiments with the people to identify appropriate institutions, technologies, methods and devices to find out an alternative path of development process. Next to the team there is yet another unit, family, which deserves my special mention here as they have allowed me free hand even without fulfilling my basic responsibilities and obligations. Hence I place on record my sincere and profound gratitude to all those who love my work and cooperate with me to strive towards perfection in all my tasks.

G. Palanithurai

CONTENTS

1
Introduction

Governance, and good governance are repeated words and some time concepts both to politicians and academics in the recent years. It is always a disease which has afflicted the Indian ruling elites to look at things from the frameworks evolved by the Westerners. Whether it is federalism or democracy or decentralization of powers or people's participation or corruption or good governance, our academics and ruling elites would look into it only after the pronouncements made from the west. Today, good governance is a much debated topic in India. Yet one would be puzzled while looking into the functioning of our democracy. In the governing process much has been debated on the structural arrangement which we have for governance in India. The discussions and deliberations are always centring around the ruling elite with a presumption that for good governance, change in the ruling class is enough. There is yet another belief that the people have nothing to contribute for governance and they are only receivers of benefits from the governing elites through the government by its allocations. People have got many things to contribute for good governance. So far they have not been tapped or utilised or even recognised. What all the ills we find in the governing process today are only with the institutions or in the ruling class and not with the people. And if at all anything is wrong in the society it is due to the percolation of the implications and consequences of the actions of the government. To set right the maladies in the existing system of governance any imported framework would not be useful and hence time has come to find out frameworks from the Indian tradition. In this regard, all the essays in this handy volume are useful.

In the essay entitled "Resilience of Indian Democracy", I brought out new propositions for further examination that the Indian democracy has still vibrancy and salience despite the poor performance of the ruling class and the resilience of Indian democracy is the outcome of the people's matured democratic actions in the political system which is contradictory to the established theories of democracy in the west. It is indicated that people have more maturity than our ruling elites. Indian parliamentary democracy provides enough scope for evolving new frameworks and theories. The new exercise could be done more comprehensively by the Indian academics who have deep acumen in our tradition and culture. It is demonstrated in the article that the system has got all required resilience to administer development. But the individuals who operate the system lack values and hence all the ills. But the socio-cultural moorings of the people have helped the system without perpetuating violence.

It is not the system which failed the people, it is the people who operate the system are at fault. All that India needs is a value profile for everyone. The values that had been evolved during the freedom struggle have been discarded. Even then the Indian political system has got the resilience of democracy. It needs reform periodically.

"Elections, Issues and Options" is a working paper written at the time of twelfth general Election to highlight some of the basic issues of our electoral process. People have been oriented to perceive that election is the only aspect governing the process of democracy. People have been made to forget that election is one of the aspects of democratic governance. It is highlighted that people have given mandate to the political parties to govern the country through the election for a period of five years but political parties, without performing their obligations and respecting the mandate, have come for election. When the eventuality comes, it is the responsibility of the ruling elites to evolve a suitable framework to overcome the eventuality. But in the Indian context, it is a repeated observation that ruling elites have failed the people and the people have managed the affairs smoothly through the options given to them.

Democracy is a finer form of governance which needs more number of capacitated individuals to participate in the governing process at different levels. In India, people have not been involved in the governing process and by which people have been incapacitated by the governing elites systematically through the establishment of an absolute State system which has been a subject of debate as total State system. The political parties have been moved into a pattern by which people have been oriented to look into the non-issues and relegating the issues to the background. Now people have a different mind-set, and this mind-set will not perceive the real problems of the society. Poverty, illiteracy, ignorance, insanitation, child labour, female infanticide, unemployment, under-employment and unemployability will be perpetuated forever. Non-issues have got prominence and the same will continue to get prominence. To alter the mind-set of the people an array of steps had been found out in the analysis. Need of the hour is recognition of the people and their capacity. Handing over responsibilities to the people to tackle the problems with the available devices known to them will be the next step.

Yet another essay "Election is an Expression of Feelings" focuses its attention on determining the quality of democracy through the election. Each and every election people give direction to leaders and parties but it seems that both leaders and parties have not learnt any lesson from the people. Now people are witnessing frequency of election not periodical election which will result in loss of faith in political parties on the part of the people. Proper understanding of the people's expression of feeling in the electoral process by the political parties will alone redeem the situation.

Politicians are used to give interpretation to the results of the election to their own advantage without looking into the reality. People's participation and non-participation in the electoral process have several meanings and underpinnings. The tumultuous change in every aspect of the society, polity and economy complicates the problem further beyond the normal comprehension of the same by the academics. Politicians, administrators and intellectuals are engrossed only in crises management and not in administering development. Crises have crept into the party, community, society and government.

There is yet another serious issue affecting Indian parliamentary democracy. People are made to believe that government is a provider and people are only to receive benefits and services from the government. Despite the proliferation of government departments and officials, people's demands and aspirations could not be met and as a result people have developed an anti-establishment sentiment. Thus the State has conceded its failures and it takes earnest endeavour to find out an alternative structural arrangement to cope with the rising expectations of the people. The above posited questions have been discussed in this chapter.

"Participatory Governance" is an article highlighting the emergence of an alternative to the existing institutional arrangement. It is unfortunate that our academics who have been trained in the liberal school believed that participatory governance is the model evolved in the west and hence they advocate that it could be adopted in Indian context. Before the advent of parliamentary democracy, people in India as a community participate in the activities of the community to tackle the problems of the community. The continuous proliferation of institutional arrangement has complicated the State and society by multiplying the problems. The basic problems and issues which the Indian society and State face cannot be solved by the institutional mechanism devised by the government. They will be tackled only by the involvement of the masses. In the fifty years of governance the sense of community has disappeared and individuality has been developed and as a result one could see the individuals in the society, not the community. Hence it is indicated that the need of the hour is a new thinking on the part of every individual with regard to structure of governing institutions and style of governance.

Society in the rural areas has to be reconstructed. From the days of M.K. Gandhi to the period of Rajiv Gandhi everyone accepted if there is no constructive work today there won't be any community tomorrow. Yet constructive activities were not carried out as a movement. Time has come to make an open statement that the role of the government has to be redefined as the state has lost its relevance in performing the development functions. Weeding out the ills and adding new features to the rural community life would bring needed development which will be sustainable in nature. The State initiated activities in the past fifty years have increased the malaises and hence it is all the more important to have a mass movement to eliminate all the diseases from the communities of the rural areas. To evoke response from the people an appropriate institution could be devised with so much of flexibility. It is to be seen that to what extent the newly created institutions are vested with powers. As long as the institutions are made as people's institutions, delivery of goods is ensured. The institution of the people alone can perform its functions under the control of the people. How institutions are brought under the control of the people, has been discussed in the chapter entitled "Rural Reconstruction and Public Participation."

The present trend of growth and development has to be seen in the context of the transformation that takes place in the rural areas. The depletion of natural resources, pollution of natural resources, exploitative economic culture, consumeristic culture, intense social tension and conflict and conflicting cultural values have altered the mind-set of the people. To bring a needed change in the rural society, an action frame has been suggested in the article entitled "A Framework for Reconstruction of Villages."

The article entitled "Struggling Grassroots Democracy in Indian Society" brings out the context, content and implications of the 73rd Amendment to the Constitution of India. Mere constitutional amendments cannot bring any substantial change in the society. It is only a framework and the basic elements of the constitutional amendment have to be incorporated in the provincial Acts also. Main provisions of both central and State Acts have to be understood properly by the people. This essay underlines the ongoing process of decentralization of power and indicates the deterrents present in the process of decentralization of power. A case (Tamil Nadu) has been taken to demonstrate the ongoing process. It has been demonstrated in this essay that how not to implement Panchayati Raj could be learnt from Tamil Nadu. There is a vast gap between the intention of the leaders who brought the 73rd amendment to the Constitution of India and the leaders who are implementing the same at the grassroots level. What should be done to implement the new panchayati system has been suggested in this article.

Yet another issue "Perception of the Leaders" has been discussed seriously in the article entitled "Conflicting Roles in Representative Institutions." Administration faces a very serious crisis in the roles of the representatives of the people. From local bodies to national parliament, representatives have been elected by the people. Representatives of national parliament, representatives of State legislatures and representatives of local bodies have distinct roles to perform in the respective institutions on the issues allocated to each of the three institutions. But unfortunately the present context projects a view that all representatives of all the three institutions are performing the same set of functions. In Indian context the representatives have been given some executive functions also by earmarking resources for the development of their constituencies. Thus the role conflict is being witnessed everywhere among the representatives of the three bodies, namely, parliament, legislature and local bodies. MPs have earmarked resources, MLAs have resources and local body leaders have also resources for constituency development activities and they are all being executed in the field. The representatives are so busy in doing this function and forgetting the original function of these institutions. Every representative is interested in meeting the local needs of the people. But at the same time there is no coordination among the representatives of the people who are implementing programmes. By doing so one would find the gap between increasing unmet needs and increasing allocation of resources to solve the problems. Moreover, our legislature and parliament take the executive powers. All those issues have been discussed in this article and solutions suggested.

"Self-Governance Sans Controls" is an important essay which deals with the attempts of the government at the state level to make the local body institutions as implementing agency to implement the government programmes instead of making them as institutions of self-governance. In the context of the establishment of local bodies with adequate powers and responsibilities to meet the basic needs of the people, it would be proper on the part of the federal and State governments to keep themselves away from proliferating more and more schemes. But in reality both the federal and State governments are evolving more and more new schemes and handing them over to local bodies for implementation. This trend has led to a feeling among the elected local body leaders that local bodies are only to implement the schemes and programmes of the government. Here also suggestions have been made to change the mind-set and to make the panchayats as people's panchayats so that they can be turned into institutions of self-governance.

"Corruption" is a major phenomenon which rocks the very foundations of democratic polity in India. Though it is a world-wide phenomenon, it has got serious implications in a society like ours. Everyone talks about corruption despite the presence of institutional mechanism to contain it and obviously it is rampant everywhere. Corruption cannot be eliminated and contained by the mere seminal discussions held in the public fora. It should have an action frame and it needs honest individuals to carry out certain actions. People are very serious at higher levels as funding agencies have been sending warning signals to the government that funding for development works would not be possible unless corruption is contained. It is not a new phenomenon. It is an age-old phenomenon which had not been considered seriously so far.

To give shape to the deliberated ideas in the fora, an attempt has been made in a small village through the panchayat. It has been working well and hence the Vadugampadi gram panchayat micro experiment on containing corruption has been reported in this essay under the caption "Containing Corruption : A Micro Experiment."

"Capacitization for Local Governance" is a report prepared from the training conducted for gram panchayati presidents of Dindigul and Sivagangai districts in Tamil Nadu. Success of the new institutional arrangement depends not only on devolution of adequate powers but also on enhancing the capacity of the leaders to discharge the responsibilities as per the powers devolved to them. Though the cry for more powers is in the agenda of the local body leaders, it is also seen simultaneously whether the leaders of the local bodies are having adequate capacity to perform their role and functions. The Ministry of Rural Areas and Employment, Government of India has given the responsibility of building up the capacity of the leaders at gram panchayat level to Gandhigram Rural Institute. While carrying out the task of conducting capacity building exercise for gram panchayat leaders, the perception and objectives of the leaders have also been elicited from them. The report is primarily prepared to make out the impact of the training. The report has brought out plethora of problems they face while performing their role and functions. It requires a lot more actions from the federal and State governments to make the local body institutions really self-governing institutions. It is an eye-opener for all. How the actual struggle is going on in the rural areas, while transferring power, has been highlighted in this report.

"People's planning Exercise in a Gram Panchayat" is again reporting of a planning committee meeting held in a gram panchayat which has been the experimental gram panchayat of the Gandhigram Rural Institute. It is in a telegraphical form as it is only a preliminary meeting to assess the needs of the people. It is interesting to note that people have more problems and issues and equally they have solutions too. Moreover, it is the belief system of the intellectuals that more amount of resources are needed to meet the needs of the people. In reality it is not so. From the people's observations one would observe that to meet the needs of the people they require only guidelines or ideas to make use of the energy of the people. Further most of the problems could be tackled by the people themselves. It has been reported in this document.

Food security is another vital problem drawing the attention of all from the policy-makers to the common man at present. Debates are on to evolve a strategy to maintain a sustainable food security system in the world. "Food Security and Grassroots Governance" is an article presented in the workshop organised in Gandhigram. In this article details regarding the major activities that could be done at the panchayati level, have been discussed. It is also indicated that the concept has taken a new shape and called it as livelihood security. Livelihood security can be achieved effectively at the grassroots level through the new panchayati system as all those issues have been included as subjects in the eleventh schedule. This aspect has been discussed in this article.

Ethnic movement in Tamil Nadu drew the attention of the scholars of the western countries for evolving frameworks and theories on ethnicity. In the course of years very many theoretical postulates have been developed. Repeated tests of the postulates on ethnicity in Tamil Nadu have indicated the faulty conceptualization of the western scholars on Dravidian Movement. The fast changes in the Dravidian Movement in the past three decades in the political process of the province have negated the principles which have been evolved over a period of five decades. The article entitled "The Paradox of an Ethnic Movement" is the result of an analysis of the ongoing transformation of the ethnic political parties in the Indian political scenario in the backdrop of the market economy. It has many new informations and it lends itself to evolving new propositions and postulates.

Thus this collection provides enough input for evolving alternative path of development. Some of the key issues have been discussed and suggestions have been carried out at micro level on an experimental basis. Theories and technical jargons have been avoided purposely as these ideas should reach the common readers. Many contentious issues have been discussed but no fruitful suggestions have been arrived at. These articles would provide stimulus and further impetus for further discussion and exploration.

2
Resilience of Indian Democracy

John Stuart Mill, an exponent and an authority on representative institutions of modern democracy, subtly expressed his apprehension over the possibility of success in the functioning of parliamentary institutions in plural societies. He remarked that the deeply divided communities on ethnic basis will not sustain parliamentary democracy.[1] It was further strengthened by Lucian W. Pye by bringing enough evidences to portray that the political process and performances of the democratic institutions are influenced by ethnic considerations. Thus the society which is deeply divided, on caste and communal considerations, will not have the resilience to absorb the finer elements of the democratic institutions in the body politic.[2] Yet the newly liberated nations of Asia and Africa ventured into the adoption of parliamentary democracy which is alien to their political culture. While considering the level and nature of the political culture of these nations, adoption of parliamentary institutions seemed to be a risky venture. Notwithstanding the high amount of risk, the political pandits of the Afro-Asian nations decided to go in for parliamentary democracy with a hope to change the attitude of the people suitable to handle parliamentary institutions effectively to deliver the goods. The task of the nations at the dawn of Independence was to change the type of political culture from parochial to participative in the course of years to sustain parliamentary democracy. Today, the growing crises in governance in many Afro-Asian countries have moved the State away from parliamentary democracy. Yet, India remains in the domain of parliamentary democracy.[3]

The Problem

While looking back on the performance of parliamentary democracy in the fifty years since Independence with a set of values which Indian polity had evolved during the freedom struggle under the leadership of M.K. Gandhi, we have to ponder over our failures and the damages done to the democratic institutions. Yet India can be proud of keeping the institutions alive, functional and vibrant to meet the challenges, pulls and pressures given by various segments of the human collectivities formed on the basis of ethnic considerations.[4] Equally, the achievements made in the field of agriculture, education, industry, technology and science in India have created a perception among the foreigners that India has achieved things in decades whereas the developed countries took centuries. Our achievements and performances have not been properly realized by the Indian masses.[5] *Hawalas*, scams, forgeries, political brokerages, mafia politics, bureaucratic corruption have drawn the attention of the people. People have been oriented to look at the drawbacks and shortcomings only and not the positive dimensions of the system. The above-mentioned events have given a signal that the crises have crept into the governance and the governability is at stake and thereby the representative institutions have lost their credibility.[6] Yet, the recent events such as booking of politicians and officials for their involvement in corruption by the intervention of the judiciary and other independent agencies like CBI suggest that the institutions are alive with adequate power and authority to deal with the problems. Against this background one should find answer to the question whether the functioning of parliamentary democracy in India has the resilience to cope with the existing crises.

The Issues Examined

India's democratic institutions continue to function. Federal and State Governments are stable from Kashmir to Kanya Kumari despite violent social conflicts. General elections have been conducted at regular intervals even in the disturbed areas. Social conflicts are so acute in many parts of the country and yet, they have not led to a breakdown of the economic order. Ministries have been formed and expanded, transactions have been carried out in the authoritative bodies at different levels to evolve policies, decision and to allocate resources to administer development. Political parties by increasing their numbers have aggregated and articulated the grievances of the people. Public grievances have been projected and processed in the legislative institutions for decision-making. On most occasions, the quantum of grievances has outstripped the capacity of the institutions. Apart from the political parties, both national and regional, a variety of groups, reference groups and pressure groups have been organized to articulate the grievances of the people and thereby gradually all segments of the society have been brought into the political system.[7] Occurrence of large-scale conflicts in Indian society is not the result of the Indian State System. They are outcome of the decisions and policies of the federal and provincial governments. Gradually, all social groups have been brought into the Indian political system as participants.[8]

Role of the Press

The press, the fourth estate, is vital for any democracy. Ever since Independence, freedom of the press was maintained in India except for a period of two years during emergency. The press played a vital role to educate the people, politically and socially. Through the media, information relating to development is disseminated thereby kindling the aspirations of the people. Expression of grievances through organizations has to be considered as a positive one as people have faith in the State and they expect development initiatives from the government.

Judiciary as a Protector

Judiciary is yet another organ protecting the democratic institutions by its intervention as and when they drift away from the basic principles. While taking action against the individuals, groups and organisations in the event of failure of other institutions such as Legislature and Executive, Judiciary has demonstrated that it has got the power, authority and strength to protect the parliamentary democracy in India. Through judicial activism all corrupt politicians are exposed to the people.

Far-reaching Changes

Executive institutions have been expanded to meet the increasing demands of the public and thereby government institutions have been multiplied to the extent of taking away the minimum responsibilities of the citizens and the community. Thus the government is made a big one.[9] Governmental institutions have been functioning in a given environmental setting. There will always be an interaction between the environment and the institutions of the government. Positive environmental conditions will always help the institutions to perform their functions effectively and efficiently. Indian environmental conditions such as parochial political culture of the people, poor commitment of the people towards the democratic institutions, absence of national pride, political apathy and passive attitude of the people towards the political institutions have affected the democratic institutions substantially in their performance.[10] Yet our parliamentary democracy has produced far-reaching changes in all spheres of the society, polity and economy of India. What we witness today in our society, polity and economy is the result of the performance of the parliamentary institutions.

One should look at growth from the perspective of the rate of growth and not the exact point of growth. Everybody is critical of the rate of growth of our population. The increase in the population has a direct bearing on the effective health policies pursued by the Government of India. In building up educational institutions, India has surpassed even the USA. In fifty years, it has established 248 universities and likewise an increasing number of colleges. India has the third largest scientific manpower. It has the eighth largest industrial power and potentiality. There are hundred million members brought to the middle class in India who have become the consuming public providing a stable market base for a growing economy. The bank deposits in the country have risen from Rs. 5,000 crore in 1970 to over Rs. one lakh crore in 1990. India, which did not produce even a safety-pin in 1947, is now producing locomotives, aeroplanes and computers. The Green Revolution which only covers part of the country has increased food production from 50.8 million tonnes in 1950-51 to 185 million tonnes on 1995-96. The investment climate in our country is so reassuring that industrialists of many foreign countries are forging collaborations daily with their Indian counterparts.[11] All these developments could be seen from the perspective of the colonial background. The growing demand for decentralization of power is the outcome of the massive expansion of the government machinery. The fast development in various sectors could not be followed effectively by the people since their level of understanding and awareness about the political system and government institutions are poor and as a result India witnessed large-scale corruption, scams and *hawalas*. Yet these malfunctioning and exploitative activities could be effectively checked through various constitutionally available devices.

Public Mobilization

The ever-growing demands of the human collectivities and formation of organizations on ethnic lines are the result of increasing political mobilization of the people by the political parties and the policies of the government.

In the political process of the nation for the past five decades, people have been oriented politically with the help of the mass media. The mass communication strategies adopted by the political parties have yielded good results in creating political awareness and the people have formed political organizations to express their grievances.[12] The ever-growing voice of the minorities in the social and political system for equity and social justice is the result of the policies pursued by the government for the last fifty years.

The emergence of more number of social groups based on caste is also the result of the efforts of the governments in advancing the equalization process.[13]

Federalism and Coalition Politics

Once the nation was worried about the development of regional political parties on the national political scene. But when the nation witnessed the failure of the national political parties to become the ruling party at the centre, the regional political parties joined together and developed a national perspective to form a government at the centre in collaboration with national political partics. Ideologically, all the political parties in the ruling United Front at the centre are having conflicting postures and yet, they joined together to give a government to the people through a Common Minimum Programme. In the States, more number of sub-regional groups have come up at the grassroots level. Coalition governments have been formed in West Bengal, Kerala, Maharashtra and UP. West Bengal has shown the model to the nation by its success.

The ongoing experiment of coalition government is another milestone in the modern political history of India. Theoretically, even the survival of parliamentary institutions in India has been questioned in the context of plurality of the society, but the nation is poised for yet another development, namely, coalition government. European governments have been experimenting consociational democracy and the same could be experimented in India also. The theories that have been developed over the years about the functioning of democracy in plural societies have not been confirmed in the case of India as it has projected new propositions for theorization and has been maturing stage by stage.

Religion, culture, language, region and caste are always acting as instruments in forming identities for socio-political activities but they will not help to form violent political events as the values which the people have cherished are not violence-pronc.

Integrated Analysis

For a long time, people used to ask the question : After Nehru, who ?, after Indira, who ? and after Rajiv, who ? with a belief that Indian democracy relies on personality, not on principles and ideology.[14] The successful completion of five-year term of office by P.V. Narasimha Rao as Prime Minister of a minority government has proved that it is not personality that matters. There is a yet another event— the selection of a candidate for the top post of the country, namely, the President of the Indian Republic. The political parties, which have contending approaches and conflicting ideologies, have come together to select a person based on consensus showing the maturity of the Indian system. There is yet another belief that people are used to accept the dictates of the dominant personalities of the political system of India. This belief was disproved in the post-emergency general election which reflected the wrath of the people in the form of ballot, by routing the ruling party in 1977. People's attachment to democracy was revealed through the ballot throughout the country.

People consider election as an effective instrument to ventilate their feelings. Because of militancy, it was believed that election could not be conducted in Punjab, Kashmir and Assam. Despite this apprehension, these States went to polls. Elections are the regular feature of Indian Democracy. In the Indian context, the State has expanded its way over the individuals beyond its limit to the level of declaring that it is almost a total State system.[15] But the mass movements based on various identities work against the expansion of State power and the State is unable to contain the mass movements. There was no other alternative except opting for decentralization of power to reduce the crisis in governance.

There is another reason for the upkeep of democratic institutions in India. The vastness of the country and the multiple social divisions have not provided scope for any individual or group to tilt the balance from democracy to dictatorship or any other form. Moreover, the British had left many legacies of which Parliament, a federal structure, an independent Judiciary, a nationally recruited bureaucracy, electoral procedures, a free press and independent political parties are important. They have taken root in the country and hence these institutions withstand all types of pressures.

Political institutions are made distinct from state institutions.[16] Likewise equilibrium has been maintained in the relationship between the States and the Centre and the States by various social groups. The social contradictions have never allowed the States to move beyond the capacity of the Centre. All violent social conflicts are the result of the continuous implementation of welfare policies and programmes by the federal and state governments. These conflicts have never affected economic growth. It is demonstrated that the system has got all resilience which is needed to administer development. But the individuals, who operate the system, lack values and hence all the ills. But the socio-cultural moorings of the people have helped the system without perpetuating violence.

It is not the system which failed the people, it is the people who operate the system who are at fault. All that India needs is a value profile for all. The values that had been evolved during the freedom struggle have been discarded. Hence Indian political system has got the resilience of democracy. It needs reform periodically.[17]

Conclusion

The Indian sub-continent by its experiment in parliamentary democracy gives scope for evolving new frameworks and theories. It is beyond doubt that the Indian experience in democratic governance has altered the proposition and framework of John Stuart Mill, Almond Lucian W. Pye, Harry Eckstein and Slig S. Harrison that the plural societies will not sustain democratic institutions. The social and cultural conditions seemed to disturb the normal functioning of parliamentary institutions. But in reality, in the Indian context, they help the parliamentary institutions to accommodate more number of social groups into their fold by modifying the system into consociational democracy. The very sustenance of democratic institutions show the success of Indian polity. But at present, Indian political system has posited two more options—minority government and coalition government. It emerged successfully in experimenting a minority government during the P.V. Narasimha Rao regime. The coalition experiment is on and it has to be watched and evaluated in the years to come. The changes that took place in Indian polity and society warranted a new theoretical framework to explain the functioning of the Indian political system. Indian democracy may have several drawbacks and yet it has got enough resilience to withstand pressure and to keep democracy alive by its elastic nature. By evolving a value profile in the political system, most of the crises could be solved. Indian democracy is seen as a wonder and it will continue to be so in the years to come.

Notes and References

1. John Stuart Mill, *Considerations on Representative Government*, New York:Liberal Arts Press, 1958, p. 230.
2. Lucian W. Pye, "Identity and the Political Culture", in Leonard Binder *et al.*, *Crises and Sequences in Political Development*, Princeton : Princeton University Press, 1971, p.117.
3. Atul Kholi, *Democracy and Discontent : India's Growing Crisis of Governability*, Cambridge : Cambridge University Press, 1991.
4. Myron Weiner, *The Indian Paradox*, New Delhi : Sage Publications, 1989.
5. Garry Jacobs, N. Krishnamurthy and N. Ramakrishnan, *Kamadhenu*, Madras : Southern Publications, 1988.
6. G. Palanithurai, *Indian Polity : Myth and Reality*, New Delhi : Kanishka Publishers and Distributors, 1989.
7. Zoya Hasan, S.N. Jha and Rasheeduddin Khan (eds.), *The State, Political Process and Identity : Reflections on Modern India*, New Delhi : Sage Publications, 1989.
8. Javeed Alam, "Political Articulation of Mass Consciousness in present day India" in Zoya Hasan, S.N. Jha and Rasheeduddin Khan (eds.), *op. cit.*, pp. 237-55.
9. Milton J. Esman, "The maturing of development administration", *Public Administration and Development*. Vol. 8, No. 2 (1988), pp. 125-34.
10. India's political culture could be determined as a parochial subject political culture. For more details, see G. Palanithurai,

People's Perception of Politics : An Indian Perspective, New Delhi : Kanishka Publishers and Distributors, 1995.

11. Garry Jacobs, N. Krishnamurthy and N. Ramakrishnan, *op. cit.*, p. 5.
12. Hartmann Paul, B.R. Patil and Anita Dighe, *The Mass Media and Village Life : An Indian Study*, New Delhi : Sage Publications, 1989.
13. For more details see G. Palanithurai and R. Thandavan (eds.), *Perspectives on Indian Regionalism*, New Delhi : Kanishka Publishers and Distributors, 1992.
14. Welles Hangen, *After Nehru Who?*, London : Rupert Hart Davis, 1963; P. Tharyan, *India:The Critical Decade After Nehru*, New Delhi : Sterling Publishers, 1974.
15. Ramshay Roy and R.K. Srivastava, *Dialogues on Development: The Individual Society and Political Order*, New Delhi : Sage Publications, 1986, pp. 69-83.
16. Prime Minister I.K. Gujral's speech in parliament on the motion for vote of confidence to prove his majority in the House on 22-04-1997.
17. G. Palanithurai, 1993, *op. cit.*, pp. 29-40.

3
Elections, Issues and Options

Introduction

Elections are routine in the democratic process of a nation. Who wins and with what margin? evokes the curiosity of political parties and journalists. To a sensible serious-minded and committed social researcher, 'how it happens?' is more important and this determines the quality and nature of democracy. While analysing this process in a representative democracy, necessarily one has to drag in the proposition of John Stuart Mill that democratic governance is absolutely not suitable to the multi-ethnic or plural society.[1] In India democratic governance has produced several puzzles.[2] Elections have been conducted, ministries have been formed, decisions have been taken, administrative machineries have been expanded, huge amount of resources have been mobilised and allocated through legislative deliberations and approval and yet problems are mounting up even to the extent of threatening the State itself by the collectivities of the people in India.[3]

The Problems

What was going on in the country at the 12th General Election is not merely the problems akin to election. It is beyond that and more particularly the problem of governance through the established system of institutions. Nobody is sure about the arrangement that was going to emerge after the election. Every party was trying to do as much as possible to be in the race to form the government. Political arithmetics is familiar to the politicians and yet they are unable to predict and announce confidently the outcome of the voting because people's decisive action in the booth cannot be judged easily and political parties are finding it very difficult to convince the people in a particular way of thinking. Though political parties are accusing each other overtly and covertly, ultimately they are held responsible for this state of affairs. Elections are to be conducted once in five years. But elections are conducted frequently as political parties and their leaders did not understand the meaning of the verdict given by the people through the ballot. In the last three elections people have given their verdict that formation of coalition is very essential and political leaders have to learn the art of managing a coalition. Instead of learning coalition and practising coalition, the political parties are demanding the people to cast their votes in favour of a dominant political party to provide stability to the Government.[4] It is a very wrong notion that coalition is unstable and non-productive in terms of performance.[5] Moreover, political partics cannot dictate terms to the people. They have to obey the mandate of the people. When people have given their mandate in favour of coalition, the political parties which have formed the coalition and conducted the coalition government should bring success to the coalition. Coalition is more than a system of arrangement of parties to govern the society and it is simply a culture. This culture has to be evolved and the same has to be developed on a sustainable basis.

The Distant Past

During the past three general elections, people have not given a solid and comfortable majority to a single political party to govern the country. Improvements and improvisations have been made on crude coalition in all the three elections.[6] The present coalition is far better than the previous coalition in terms of its performance. This time also they are expecting a hung Parliament which necessitates a coalition arrangement. Even in the western countrics, it took several years to perlect the coalition arrangement. Ultimately coalition and minority governments have fared well than the single party dominated majority government in the western countries. Coalition can succeed in its performance. India a poor nation cannot wait for such a long time to get maturity in coalition. But then what is the way out. An alternative has to be thought of. Political parties and leaders have to seriously consider this problem, otherwise people would lose their faith in democracy altogether. Political parties are confusing the people as State is compelling them to cast their votes. Supposing people organise themselves non-politically and take a decision not to go to booth to cast their votes on the plea that they had elected the candidates for five years, why then again an election within two years? What is the answer to this question of the people? It is true that political leaders priority today is to make use of any opportunity to assume power. The political parties have a strong belief today that necessarily people have to come around to their belief system. Parties believe that by projecting the instability of coalitions, one party can get majority without knowing the emerging pattern of perception of the people about polity and society. People at present want to increase their share in the political process of the nation.[7]

It is a truism that politics has percolated to the grass-roots level and people have developed perspectives about politics. Once nationalism, nation building, and State formation gained support from the people. Slowly new concepts like ideology, regional disparities and other related issues dominated the functioning of the political parties. Later regionalism, province building, ethnicity, language and culture drew the attention of the people. Now caste and religion preoccupied the minds of the people by relegating all other concepts to the background. Polity has been so fragmented. In the years to come coalition has to be the arrangement for even provincial governments. It has come to West Bengal, Kerala, Uttar Pradesh, and Maharashtra. Experiences are demonstrating the fact that coalition can be a successful arrangement in providing a stable government and good governance. Likewise panchayats are able to function in a conglomeration of political parties joining together to administer development. When Panchayats and State Governments are successful in coalition why not the federal government? is the major question haunting the minds of the people. During the first three decades after Independence politics centred round development.[8] After 1970 politics slowly drifted away from development and mostly it is a politics of crisis in governance. In the fiftieth year while taking stock of the situation we are not able to proudly proclaim that India is able to provide basic minimum facilities to the people for a decent human life.[9] In the whole of the world largest collectivities of illiterates will be found in India in the coming century and likewise the unemployed and poverty-stricken people. Our planning, investment, implementation and evaluation of development activities have failed to produce the expected results. The question is to what extent the results have solved the human miseries? While looking at the problems in the society to be tackled in the century to come, one is doubtful whether the existing system will be successful in delivering the expected goods in the given environment.[10]

We have not learnt sufficiently from our experience during the past five decades despite witnessing many failures.[11] Basically our understanding of the issues and approaches is not reflecting the realities and as a result we could not succeed in our attempts to solve even the problems of the society..

The people of our country despite being illiterate, are aware of the functions of the State. Their demands on the State have increased the workload of the government.[12] The government is unable to meet the increased demands of the people. Repeated politicization of the people by the mobilising activities of the politicians has made them more conscious of the polity rather than the social issues confronting the society. A thorough metamorphosis of the Indian polity has been witnessed in the course of fifty years of democratic governance. By the effort of the government the expected social transformation had not been achieved as has been achieved in the field of polity.

Our polity in outer form exhibits sophistication and maturity but in inner form (in content and process) it is not matured and oriented towards development. Our political system reflects the social reality. In appearance the linkages between the social conditions and political realities are paradoxical in nature.[13] But in reality both are closely interactive mutually reflecting the backwardness in terms of their functions.

Politicians are keen in using the sentiments of the people. The elements of sentiments may be drawn from culture, language, religion, caste and so on. In India for about three decades people had been oriented on non-issues and for which large scale illiteracy and ignorance of the people have been exploited. To move closer to the people. Politicians have identified and used the traditional elements which are so attractive but non-productive and yet people are oriented again and again on sentimental non-issues for political mobilization. In this process of political mobilization and orientation, issues have been relegated to the background.

The Issues

Today issues are not different from the age of Gandhi. Gandhi had evolved a programme of action to attack all those issues in the Indian society under the caption "Constructive Programme". Schemes are many and yet problems are on the increase and intensity of the problems has also increased. It is still true that India lives in villages and Agriculture keeps the people alive. But micro economy, ecology, environment, sanitation, water supply and agriculture do not find substantial attention in the policy-making arena as the policy-making centres are fully dominated by the thought process of urban-oriented intellectuals and industrialists. Major issues confronted by the Indian National Movement headed by M.K. Gandhi still continue with the same intensity which needs the attention of the policy-makers.

Indian politics has become election-oriented and not development-oriented. Development issues do not find a place in the electioneering. Non-issues have been projected and this created a sort of apathy among the voters. People in the villages do not find employment opportunity for at least 250 days in a year to earn enough to manage their affairs for the whole year. Since agriculture was not a priority area for the government, it became a cultural activity of the farmers. Agriculturists are facing plethora of problems from input to output. To redeem the life of the farmers, State's attention is imperative. For the poor in the villages food security is a major issue which needs immediate attention. Villages are in the thick of environmental problems. There is no proper sanitation in the rural areas. Presence of illiteracy pulls the people towards backwardness despite huge investment in the educational sector. There is no proper management of educational system in our country and as a result people are compelled to be in the clutches of the private institutions to educate their wards in the rural areas. Providing drinking water facility to all the people in India is still a dream. But attempts are on in this regard. Providing health facilities to all the people in India requires a huge amount of money. Even after providing such facilities, people are not satisfied with the facilities provided by the Government as they (Personnel) are not accountable to the people. The built-up machinery to administer development for people has turned towards themselves and against the people and as a result, the people have developed an anti-establishment sentiment which is considered as a dangerous phenomenon for a healthy democracy. Political parties continuous mobilisation of the people for political process has diverted the people from community life to individuals and individualistic individuals have come together as stake-holders to get benefits in the share of the decisions, policies and money allocation under any one of the traditional symbols namely religion, region, caste, language and culture. Yet the traditional value system though has developed cracks internally, and it has not developed overtly to break the traditional structures and thus Indian villages are in the grip of casteist forces which are not functioning in harmonious arrangement but in conflicting situations.[14] Though people accept the caste identity, they do not subscribe to the principle of *Varna* of *Hindutva*. Development of media and its network in the society, has successfully established their control over the mind-set of the people. Media has created a revolution in their thought process especially in raising their expectations. The craze for materialism has pushed the people to make use of any opportunity to make money and in this process, the value system, that had been followed for several centuries, has been totally relegated to the background.[15] Resource sharing is a major exercise done by the community which creates lot of division among the community. In the fast changing political scenario, symbols do not find anchorage in the minds of the people. Identity moves from religion to region, region to language, language to culture, culture to caste and so on and so forth. The fast switching over of loyalty and identity of the people from one symbol to another to get maximum share in allocation of resources in the governing process has not established peace and development. Disharmony prevails everywhere as people are in transition from one identity to another.

The changing value system has helped the people to move faster in changing their identities as change of identity has not been visualized seriously and negatively. Hence it is a major struggle for the mobilizers to organize and mobilize the people for a specific task as people are on the move. Fifty years of political mobilization process accelerated by the political parties by criticising each other for the misdeeds has created a belief system among the people that politics is a profession by which one can earn money and hence expecting monetary benefits from the politicians and the representatives of the people has not been considered as unethical. To woo the people again and again to keep themselves in power politicians have changed the government from facilitator to provider status which ultimately built up the organisations of the Government to the extent of making the people idle by taking away even minimum functions of the community.

To carry out all the programmes and schemes to meet the expectations, money flow has been increased in quantum which drew the attention of all. The changing value framework of the people, increasing expectations of the people, massiveness of the Government machinery, increasing cost of politics, widening gap between the people and the government, and increasing amount of money in the flow process of the government system have paved way for corruption from the level of leakage to seepage. No one single party or politician is responsible for it. The entire system of governance, all political parties and belief system of the people and their linkages with international system are responsible for this state of affairs.

The present crises in India whether they are in the domain of population explosion or health sector, or educational sector, or industrial sector or agriculture sector or management sector, attract the foreign companies for intervention only based on the opportunities they find in India in all our crises. While finding solutions to all these problems one would find enormous opportunities for work and profit. But Indian politicians, bureaucrats and even people are always on the side of the problems and not on the side of the solutions. For the problems India confronts, enormous amount of money is not the imperative need. It is needed to some extent and not to the extent of the projections made by the politicians. The achievements we have made on different fronts are not due to the money brought from the funding agencies of the West. They are all due to the resources mobilised internally. The design we have today to improve our economy will pave way only for utilising the resources available here to make profit for the foreign companies and the Indian rich. This design cannot eliminate poverty from our soil. The facilities we create in the new design of our economy need capacitated individuals to accelerate the economic growth. But our people's capacity is not in tune with the expectations of the visionaries of new economic development.

Hence one would find a perfect mismatch between the available capacity and the expected capacity of the people to move into the framework of new economy. In the process of unutilized human force, society would witness only social tension. Success of any State depends on how best the State is able to use the energy of the people through its policy options. Policy framework of the government should always be in tune with the capacity of the people. Here it is appropriate to refer to a pertinent event from Indian history. Gandhiji had developed a belief and proposition contradictory to the belief of the elites of the Indian National Congress. He believed that enormous amount of human energy is untapped in India and that could be harnessed to liberate the nation through a system which is acceptable to the Indian ethos and belief system of the people. He succeeded in his attempt. After Gandhi, no systematic effort was made to galvanise the energy of the people, only at a limited level energy of the farmers had been utilised through Green Revolution. Beyond this no systematic effort was made to galvanise the energy of the people.

Developed nations have increased the capacity of the people and thereby the capacitated individuals had been fully utilised by the State through its policy options. One would find a perfect match between the policy options and the capacity of the people. In India problems are so acute in the villages which need capacitated individuals to tackle them. Series of programmes have been executed only by the individuals who have very poor capacity. Concentration of capacitated individuals is more at the higher level and less at the lower level when problems are so acute. Whether it is a Primary School or Primary Health Centre or Block Development Office, everywhere one would find mediocres to tackle the problems. People with skill and acumen would prefer higher positions and high salaried business ventures. Hence migration of the rural people to urban centres for higher level activities is inevitable. To redeem the situation issues are to be cleared and solutions are to be sought and action programme has to be evolved.

What is to be Done?

(a)	Population explosion	:	to be reduced
(b)	Agriculture	:	Lands to be distributed.
		:	Improve the farm sector.
		:	Bring more lands under cultivation.
		:	To be developed to achieve food security.
		:	To compete in the world market also.

(c) Industry. (Cottage and Small)	:	To provide employment opportunity.
	:	To harness the local skills.
	:	To increase the productive skill.
(d) Insanitation and protected water supply	:	Sanitary condition has to be improved. Harnessing local technology to convert the night-soil into compost manure. Safe water to all.
(e) Shelter	:	To provide shelter to all families.
(f) Education	:	Make use of the educational institutions on an extension basis to eradicate illiteracy as a crash programme.
	:	Implementing new education policy rigorously
	:	People-oriented educational system.
	:	Local level control over the educational institutions.
(g) Health	:	Health for all in 2000 AD. Health facilities have to be managed by the local level institutions.
(h) Environment	:	Environmental consciousness of the people has to be used to protect the environment.

The abovc-stated issues are basic which need immediate attention of the new government. The rest are not so critical and the basic issues are to be solved only by the people through their own organisations and thereby the energy of the people could be used. High employment potentiality is available in the rural areas while tackling problems in sanitation, water supply, health sector, agriculture, cottage and small industry, housing and environmental sectors. People's knowledge, people's energy and people's skill could be harnessed. By doing so people cannot be used as pawn in the political game as their energy, skill and knowledge are fully utilised to make profit for the people themselves. Peace could be achieved only through the constructive work.

Whichever party or combine forms the new government, it should take initiative to make use of the energy, skill and knowledge of the people. They have to govern the country only on the issues and not on non-issues. Coalitions have to be made on issues and not on personalities. Constituents are to be committed towards the issues and issues are to be decided by voting ; majority opinion has to prevail. For any decision religion and caste cannot be referral points.

People's organisations have to be developed. More of the responsibilities have to be handed over to people's organisations, not to the government departments. Government departments have to be reduced. Powers of the government from federal to the State have to be reduced and give them to people's organisations.[16] Making the State so strong is need of the hour. The approach of the government has to be changed to cope up with the needs.

Notes and References

1. John Stuart Mill. *Considerations on Representative Government*, New York : Liberal Arts Press, 1958.
2. Arend Lijphart, *The Puzzle of Indian Democracy : A Reinterpretation*, New Delhi : Rajiv Gandhi Institute for Contemporary Studies, 1994.
3. Atul Kohli, "Crisis of Governability", in *Politics in India* (ed.), Sudipta Kaviraj, Delhi : Oxford University Press, 1997.
4. BJP contested the election with a major slogan "Stability".
5. For more details about the success of minority governments and coalitions see Storm Kaare, "Party Goals and Government Performance in Parliamentary Democracies", *The American*

Political Science Review, 79 : 3 (Sep, 1985), pp. 738-754.

6. G. Palanithurai, *Indian Polity : Myth and Reality*, New Delhi : Kanishka Publications, 1996.
7. It is an era of people's participation in governing process of the nation. For more details see. T.K. Oommen, "Changing Paradigms of Development: The Evolving Participatory Society", *Journal of Social and Economic Development*, Vol.1, No. 1 (Jan-Jun, 1998), pp. 35-45.
8. Slig S. Harrison, *India : The Most Dangerous Decades*, Princeton:Princeton University Press, 1960.
9. For more details about India's position in delivering services, see, UNDP. *Human Development Report, 1997*. New Delhi : Oxford University Press, 1997.
10. There is no correlation between the capacity of the development functionaries and the work load in the society for development activities. For more details see International Commission on Peace and Food. *Developing Human Resourcefulness : Strategies to Eradicate Poverty in the 1990's*, California : INCPF, 1995.
11. Amartya Sen, "How India has fared" *Frontline* (Aug. 22, 1997), pp. 35-37.
12. G. Palanithurai, *People's Perception of Politics : An Indian Perspective*, New Delhi : Kanishka Publications, 1996.
13. Myron Weiner, *The Indian Paradox : Essays in Indian Politics* New Delhi : Sage Publications, 1989.
14. Jayaram and Satish Saberwal (eds.), *Social Conflict*, Delhi : Oxford University Press, 1996.
15. Paul McCarthy, *Postmodern Desire Learning from India*, New Delhi : Dromilla & Co. Publishers, 1994.
16. Ajit M. Banerjee and K.A. Chandrasekaran (eds.), *Renewing Governance : Issues and Options*, New Delhi : Tata McGraw Hill Publishing Company, Limited, 1996.

4
Election is an Expression of Feelings

Introduction

In a democratic polity, election is an instrument through which feelings and emotions of the people about the political system are expressed.[1] Election is a major exercise in which people act both individually and collectively at different levels. Victory, margin, and formation of government are the outcome of the electoral process but these aspects do not determine the quality and nature of democracy. The methodology adopted in the process of election by the parties and the people would decide the quality of democracy. Victory of candidates, margin of votes secured by the candidates to win and lose the election and the seats secured by the party or parties to form the government are only the effects of the event in election. Party's involvement in the electoral process is from selecting candidates to mobilizing the people to support the candidates of the party, Election Commission's steps from making proper arrangement for the smooth conduct of the election to supervising the whole exercise, and people's involvement from keeping themselves away from the electoral process to participating in the electioneering very actively in favour of candidates and parties apart from casting votes in the election decide the pattern of political development.[2] By carefully watching the electoral process, one can understand the perceptions of the people. In country like India, every election is significant as it has been watched carefully and analysed meticulously by the scholars of the west to identify the pattern of behaviour of the people in the electoral process to test some of the basic propositions of representative democracy. It is true that some of the general elections in India have brought out new propositions for testing and validation. In the same way XII general election has been considered as a significant event in the democratic process of the Indian polity. IX, X and XI general elections in India had not given any clear-cut majority to any political party to form a majority Government. Consensus and coalition became a reality. During the two periods minority government and coalition government ruled the country and introduced major reforms in the economy of the country.[3] Yet stability became a question in the political process. It is still doubtful whether the question of stability has any stake in the electoral politics during the XII general election. The curiosity revolves around the basic question whether India moves away from coalition politics after experimenting two coalitions or the same trend is going to continue.

The Problem

In the fifty years the political mobilization of the people through the political parties with different identities has grouped the mass very narrowly and thereby politics became fragmented. In the backdrop of the national freedom struggle political issues were considered for about a decade and later political issues were divided on ideological settings for another two decades. Later slowly politics has moved over to the domain of regional issues and now it is centring around communal issues. When communal issue is being highlighted, it refers to both casteist and regional issues. Whether people prefer secularism at the cost of stability by rejecting the party which speaks of *Hindutva* or prefer stability at the cost of secularism or prefer a combination of many at the cost of stability is the main question to be probed in this write-up.

The Context

The twelfth general election took place at a critical juncture when moral turpitude has gone down to the lowest ebb,[4] social conflict has reached its zenith,[5] corruption in public life has eaten away the vitals of our ethos,[6] irresponsibility prevails in every quarter of the society, bedlam establishes its sway over polity and society, apathy, defection, fear and uncertainty are lingering in the minds of the people. The nation is undergoing a tumultuous change in every respect and nobody knows where it is heading. Despite this high social conflict and tension democratic values are being expressed through election periodically[7] and now it has become a fun not to the people but to the politicians. This type of electoral politics cannot bring any qualitative change in the attitude of the people towards the democratic practice. Instead of timely election, people are facing frequency of election which ultimately reduces the interest and faith of the people in democracy. Once mandate is given by the people for the political parties, it is the responsibility of the political parties and the elected representatives to find out the modalities to govern the country for the stipulated period of five years. This type of election will reflect the poor understanding of the parties and leaders. Stability and instability are the creation of the parties and the representatives. People are giving mandate to the representatives for a specified period of five years.

Fixing responsibility and blaming each other for the crises will not help the system for its smooth functioning. When there is a crisis of governance, it is the responsibility of each and every representative of the people and the leaders of the party. Within eighteen months after getting the mandate of the people the political parties are again seeking the mandate from the people. The political parties are losing their credibility among the voters as they could not arrive at a decision to avoid a crisis.

The questions of stability, communalism, Ram Mandir, reservation, casteism, and Babari Masjid are not the major issues today. Poverty, unemployment, insanitation, non-availability of potable water to all citizens, non-availability of educational facilities to all the people of India, inadequate health facilities to the people, poor capacity of the people, corrupt practices in administration, polity and society, industrial stagnation, food security, sluggish bureaucracy, lethargic police administration, environmental degradation, poor law and order situation, exploitative economy, and violent social conflict in the society are the real issues to be tackled in India by the involvement of all the political parties. So far regional political parties have shifted their plank from issues to non-issues to capture power by projecting culture, language, region, and caste as factors. Now even the National political parties have started moving from issues to non-issues by projecting religion, stability, secularism, *mandir*, and a few others to capture power. From ninth general election onwards, people have decided not to give majority to any political party to form government on their own. Explanations are many for the fragmented politics. In reality, it has become necassary for the political parties to join together to put up a joint front to form the government. People have seen the one party government through their performance while they were in majority simple and absolute. For many of the ills stable governments are responsible and it has been proved beyond doubt. This is not true that coalition government will bring instability. On the other hand coalition and minority governments have fared well than the majority governments.[8]

Understanding the people's mandate by the political parties is the imperative need of the hour. In the fifty years of political mobilization done by the political parties, all negative elements of Indian democratic polity had been projected and highlighted with the simple objective of capturing power. Mutual abuses and criticisms have been perceived by the common man as the results of democratic process and thereby slowly antiestablishment sentiments have been reflected in the elections. More and more number of people have been bracketed under political parties' fold gradually and their perceptions along with non-political citizens perceptions decide the fate of the government. Party cadres are just like business partners of the corporate company working for the political profit of the party to increase socio-economic concessions for the party cadre. A stage has come to declare that Indian democracy is the government of the party cadre, for the party cadre and by the party cadre. Leaders and the cadres have no hesitation to change their sides and to cross the floor. The speed with which the leaders have crossed floors brings many surprises. People do not know how fast they are changing colours by crossing the floor. This defection from one party to another with the expectation of becoming members of authoritative bodies mars the image of the politicians. Even top level leaders have no hesitation to change their loyalty from one party to another.[9] The people are bewildered at the farce of conducting elections again and again even though mandate is given to the representatives for a period of five years. Points and counter-points are projected against each other in the course of electioneering. These projections, criticisms and arguments have not highlighted any positive aspect of democracy. Year after year quality of our democratic practice is going down. Against this background the twelfth general election is being held.

Electioneering

Alliances are forged at the national level and regional level. From the alliances one cannot make out anything regarding the perspective of either ideology or policy options. Every segment of a group or a combination is trying to gain the maximum number of seats to form the government. Anybody can be accommodated in any combine irrespective of their worthiness and backgrounds. Every unit has developed a suspicion over the other partners. Because pre-poll alliance will be to get maximum number of seats, and post poll alliance will be to share power with dominant partner of the government.

Election machinery has done its part for the smooth conduct of election. Media has done its part to mobilize the people for voting. But the political parties have adopted means only with the objective of winning the election and form the government. Violence, booth capturing and intimidation are the means adopted by the supporters of political parties, which has lowered the image of the political parties and thereby the type of political culture of our society is determined. The way in which the whole exercise is being done by the political parties indicates the subjective nature of our political culture. Normally, through the socialization process with the help of the developed media, political culture has to be improved gradually towards participative political culture. In the Indian case, it is not so. This has plunged the nation deeper into the crisis.

What Next?

There is no doubt that the nation is in crisis, not in terms of economy but in terms of governance. How governance should be made trouble-free? Today's governance is in crisis because of its bigness. Government is so big, enjoying unlimited powers, and has established its roots in each and every family in India. People of India knowingly or unknowingly are oriented to perceive government as a provider and the people are only receiver.[10] The total usurpation of the powers of the people by the State authorities has relegated the people to the background. Common man cannot understand the structure of the government offices and services.[11] The gap between the people and the ruling elite has increased enormously and thereby these governmental institutions have acquired a new status and there is no transparency in the activities of the government. Moreover, people have no control over the government and in turn Government has full control over the people.[12] Reducing the size of the government is more important. But it is a himalayan and herculean task. It should start from the Federal Government. The number of ministers have to be reduced and consequently ministerial staff and departments have to be reduced. The number of offices has to be reduced. Mere reduction in the number of offices won't help the administration. Unnecessarily created administrative structures have to be removed. Works have to be classified and accordingly works that are to be performed by the government departments have to be done by them and the rest could be given to agencies like NGO and service sectors. The same reductions have to be carried out at the regional or State level also. More works have to be attended at the lower level. While reducing the work-load of the higher echelons of government, it is necessary to find out suitable micro level organisations without cumbersome and complicated administrative procedures to perform the task of administering development.[13]

The new framework of governance stipulates less structures, simple procedures and more participation of people. Likewise the new arrangement needs a thorough change in the structure of resource mobilization for the State.[14] The present arrangement of collection and allocation of resources needs a drastic change. Mobilising the resources from below to the top and repumping the same from top to bottom has created much complications. Unnecessary tapping of resources from the people and spending the same for various activities simply because of the fact that resources are available with the State has caused much trouble in the present-day system of resource sharing.[15]

Government functions and their expenditure have to be reduced drastically. Likewise political parties' expenditures have to be chalked out carefully and scrutinized. As long as the political parties are spending huge amounts of money for their meetings and functions, corruption will continue to establish its hold over the society. Political parties should not unnecessarily mobilize the people by spending a huge amount of money fraudulently earned. There should be a check on spending of money. Fiscal discipline is not only for the government. It is for every individual, every family, every institution, and every organisation. Every village has to be connected with a communication network. All messages to the people could be given through the communication channels like radio and television and it is through these channels that thc people can be contacted by the political parties.

Steps should be taken to identify the problems affecting the people. In India, problems are less in the given framework of resources available at hand. People are not liabilities if they are capacitated properly.[16] For every problem human collectivity can find solution and not the government. Western governments have found out the ways and means to utilise the human energy to achieve development. State should have strategy to harness the energy.[17] Their charged energy has to be directed by the State to achieve higher growth through the adventuristic activities of the people. In India so far strategies have not been worked out to galvanise the energy of the people. Of course piecemeal and fragmented steps have been taken as for example through the Green Revolution farmers' energy has been utilised to increase productivity. Likewise high level energy of the entrepreneurs has been used to achieve this much of industrial growth. Thus fragmented initiatives have been taken to use the people for social reconstruction.

The problem today with us is not capital accumulation or technology; it is proper utilization of human energy for social reconstruction. The unutilised energy has been used by the political parties and social organisations for socio-political mobilization. Socio-political organisations have used the human energy for politicization and thereby the social conflict has escalated. To avoid this social conflict, human force which has been misused and misdirected, has to be properly used and for this steps have to be taken to channelise the energy for reconstruction work. To channelise the energy minimum of resources are needed. In the villages unemployed youth and women are available, school children, apart from the study hours are available for constructive work, students from higher level educational institutions, bureaucrats, government officials are available for constructive work. Volunteers of political parties are also available for this work. All these forces have to be utilised appropriately.

The Problems to be Tackled

Rural sanitation is a very big challenge to the Indian State. It is to be tackled only by the community with the involvement of the people not through the sanitation programme of the Government of India or Government of the provinces. Individuals have to be oriented to tackle this problem. Population explosion is a serious problem which is considered as a problem of the State and for which we expect policy option of the government. It would be done not through policy option but through the mass movement. By changing the mind-set of the people population explosion could be avoided. Illiteracy is yet another problem to be tackled by the educated men and women in an organised way. Environmental protection could be done by the people with an objective of developing flora and fauna and growing plants and preventing deforestation activities. Employment opportunities are to be created in the rural areas with the available skills in the villages. For many of the activities, community has to provide the resources.

The people in India have a strong belief that the State is the provider and hence it is the duty of the State to provide everything to the people. People have to elect their representatives by casting their votes whenever election comes. After the election, everything is left to the discretion of the government. For centuries, many of the activities of the modern State had been managed by the community itself. Cleanliness of the area of human settlement, providing drinking water to the people by keeping the tanks and wells clean, maintaining the common properties well for the use of the community, protecting the properties of the people, settling the disputes of the people and a number of activities had been looked after by the people themselves through their local bodies for several centuries. Now it is a thing of the past, because the modern State has taken upon itself several responsibilities from the people to reconstruct the society. The ills that were found in the society could have been set right through the people themselves by changing their mind-set. But instead of changing their mind-set they have created a new institution called State. Hence now these responsibilities of caring for the society could be taken away from the State and entrusted to the grassroots level institutions. When more powers are taken away from the State, competition for power will be reduced considerably and thereby, cost of investment in electoral politics would be reduced substantially. When investment for politics and election is reduced corruption in public life would be reduced. One would find less competition, less investment, less corruption in the political activities. Any type of coalition arrangement could be formulated in a new situation. Political partics would adjust with each other. The imperative need is restructuring the government and the entire polity by taking away more powers from the State and entrusting these powers to local bodies as responsibilities of the community at the local level.

In the 12th general election, nearly 55% of the people cast their votes. 45% of the voters did not participate in the election. Reasons may be different. Arguments could be posited either way. People who are satisfied with the existing order will not come to the booth and equally people who have their resentment with the system will also not come to the booth to cast their votes. Our analysis, interpretations, explanations revolve around the main point of 55% votes polled in the election. The expansion of the organisational structure of the political parties and the proliferation of political parties has made more and more people politically conscious. People are being branded and bracketed under different party folds. Hence 55% of votes have to be explained from the perspective of political parties' democracy. Victory and failure are decided by grouping and regrouping of political parties for electoral context.

The results of 12th general election indicated the anti-establishment sentiments throughout the country. The continuation of one party cannot be assured as was the case with the Indian National Congress in the past. People's expectations have increased as tall promises have been made to them. It is impossible for the government machinery to fulfil these promises. No representative can satisfy the demands of the constituents. Moreover, a large number of candidates who had four decades' experience in Parliament had again been given tickets. The people are fed up with the system and the people who are responsible for this type of chaos.

The new trend in Indian politics demands an alternative approach of development. People have anti-establishment sentiments. Political parties have fragmented themselves and paved way for national parties to consolidate their position. Political parties believe that there is no connection between issues and electoral verdicts. By attracting crowds and by spending money one can win the election— is a myth. Without the cooperation of the regional parties no national political party can get majority. Alliance formation plays a vital part. The new situation demands a totally new approach for consolidation. Whichever party forms the government cannot and should not toe the beaten path. A radically different approach and policy option are needed.

What People Expect?

People are tired of the political gimmicks and drama over fifty years. Their demands are very simple. Their basic needs are to be met. Their aspirations and hopes should not be belied. Their demands should be heard in a responsive way in all the offices of the government. Their representatives should not act like a party man looking after the interests of the party. They should maintain all links with people. People should not be made to meet the representatives. Representatives have to meet the people. The representatives should have clear-cut ideas on the issues of the people. The representatives of the people should not pose themselves as a distinct class and they should be one among the people. They should speak of the developmental issues rather than non-issues. People are prone to reject candidates who had been contesting the election for the fourth or fifth time without any major achievements to their credit. People reject money and muscle power silently. People demand much transparency in the activities of the government and the activities of the politicians. Hence revolutionary ideas and actions alone can reform our democracy and make our government active and vibrant.

Notes and References

1. Bernard Berelson, "Democratic Theory and public opinion" in *Political Behaviour : A Reader in Theory and Research* (eds.), Heinz Eulau, Samuel J. Eldersveld and Morris Janowitz, New Delhi : Amerind Publishing Co. Pvt. Ltd. 1972, pp. 107-15.
2. Lucian W. Pye, *Aspects of Political Development*, New Delhi : Amerind Publishing Co. Pvt. Ltd, 1972 p. 39.
3. Prem Shankar Jha, "The Five Years of Narasimha Rao". *The Hindu* (7.4.96) Sunday, p.16.
4. C. Subramaniam "An Agenda of Action - I" *The Hindu* (18.7.97).
5. Myron Weiner, *The Indian Paradox : Essays in Indian Politics*,

New Delhi : Sage Publications, 1996.

6. Prem Shankar Jha "Corruption & Nation-building", *The Hindu*, (4.9.97).
7. Yogendra Yadav, "Indian Democracy I.-II", *The Hindu*, (19.8.97).
8. Storm Kaare, "Party Goals and Government Performance in Parliamentary Democracies", *The American Political Review*, 79:3 (Sep, 1985), pp. 738-54.
9. It has been witnessed that top leaders from Indian National Congress moved over to BJP during the time of election by projecting flimsy arguments against the leadership.
10. Ajit M. Banerjee and K.A. Chandrasekaran (eds.), *Renewing Governance: Issues and Options*, New Delhi:" Tata McGraw Hill Publishing Company Limited, 1996.
11. G. Palanithurai, *People's Perception of Politics : An Indian Perspective*, New Delhi : Kanishka Publications, 1996.
12. For more details about Indian State see Zoya Hasan, S.N. Jha and Rasheeduddin Khan (eds.), *The State Political Processes and Identity: Reflections on Modern India*, New Delhi : Sage Publications, 1989.
13. New Panchayati Raj System has come to take more responsibility at the grassroot level. For more details see G. Palanithurai (ed.), *Empowering People: Issues and Solutions*, New Delhi: Kanishka Publications, 1997.
14. Raja J. Chelliah, *Towards Sustainable Growth: Essays in Fiscal and Financial Sector Reforms in India*, Delhi: Oxford University Press, 1996, pp. 139-59.
15. The resource aspect had been seriously brought to discussion by the Gandhian Economist J.C. Kumarappa and he evolved a framework for resource use by the State and community.
16. International Commission on Peace and Food, *Developing Human Resourcefulness: Strategies to Eradicate Poverty in the 1990's* California: INCPF, 1995.
17. For more details , see Indira Gandhi Memorial Trust, *Redefining the Good Society*, New Delhi: Wiley Eastern Limited, 1995

5
Participatory Governance

Introduction

India with an amalgam of human collectivities with different identities to compete with each other and sometimes in conflict to share resources in the process of authoritative allocation of values, is undergoing a tumultuous change in an unprecedented way beyond the comprehension of even the well established academics through their theories.[1] There are protagonists to appreciate the State for its impressive achievements in many fronts by projecting the data estimated by the government itself. Of course, equally there are academics and activists who have anti-establishment sentiments and projected a dismal picture of the performance of the State by indicating the increasing lawlessness of the State and the crises in governance.[2] An objective researcher who delves deep into the performance of the State has seen both dimensions more carefully to find out the onward march of the State and society.[3] While complementing the impressive performance of the State in Industrial, Agricultural, Banking, Communication, Marketing and Educational sectors, one cannot brush aside the acute problems and issues of degradation of environment, loss of moral and ethical values in the conduct of socio-political life of the people.[4]

There are of course a battery of problems which are affecting the society in more than one way. Problems akin to banking, trade and industry could be set right within a short span of time by changing the mechanism. But the environmental problems and loss of moral and ethical values in social life of the people would take a long time to recuperate from the ills and set right the maladies. To redeem the society from this disaster volley of steps have to be taken. They are to be discussed in this chapter.

The Issues

Kashmir, Punjab, Nagaland and Assam were brought under democratic rule by the involvement of the people. People's war group in Andhra Pradesh, ULFA in Assam, JKLF in Kashmir, extremists in North-Eastern provinces, sectarian and communal forces in many provinces have been causing concern to the State. Likewise keeping private army for individuals, terrorising the people through the bomb culture in Bihar and Tamil Nadu respectively questioned the governing capacity of the State governments. Moral values of the bureaucracy and ethical principles of the politicians have gone down to the lowest ebb. The achievements in the field of agriculture, industry, education and health with the massive expansion of the government departments do not match the failures. Massive failures of the State have tempted serious-minded citizens question the very purpose of the State. The State became pivotal in administering development. When more amount of failure is attributed to the State, what is the alternative available in the given framework of governance in parliamentary democracy? How all these evils could be removed from the existing system? is the concern of everybody today. This question is addressed in this article.

A Framework for Analysis

It is almost true that the democratic governments in the third world countries are always engaged in crisis management.[6] Most of the countries have drifted away from the path of parliamentary democracy. India is the only country still surviving with democratic institutions. But the living democracy has anything substantial to contribute to the society other than managing the affairs and to consolidate the State is a daunting question. Answer could be whatever we could gain for the society from the State is something people get while the State consolidates its position and expands its activities. It is axiomatic that all activities of the people should be visualised from the perspective of the State.[6] Likewise people expect that every activity of the community is in the hands of the State and it has to perform a variety of functions and thus individuals have given up slowly the functions, duties and responsibilities of the community and the State has taken all those responsibilities from the people. What the State apparatus has done during the past fifty years? State activities are always reflected through the government functions. The basic tenet of the State in the era of nation-building was that nation-states were supreme entities for the betterment of the people and State has to take initiative for the development of the people and people have to participate in the programmes of the government. Thus development is State-oriented and people will be placed at the receiving end.

The governments at various levels have acted through their agencies. Legislative institutions have to enact legislations, evolve policies, allocated resources for all development activities. All these decisions and policies will be evaluated in terms of the provisions of the Constitution by the judiciary if they are referred to for analysis and adjudication. The evolved policies, resolved decisions and allocated resources were put into action in the society by the well-established bureaucracy. Impact and implications of the decisions and policies could be seen through the reactions of the political parties and organised groups on the implemented policies and decisions. It is a continuous process.[7] In a developing society with a democratic set-up, the decisions, policies and money allocations have to reduce the political demands and to promote peace and harmony but contrary to expectation, intensity of competition for resource sharing has increased to the level of conflict among human collectivities. When number of institutional arrangements has multiplied, automatically the institutions have to tackle the problems of the people and consequently the problems will be minimised.[8] But now instead of minimising the problems the institutions of the government have increased the problems. In the process of tackling the crises, government institutions have taken the responsibilities of the citizens. Thus it is a process of expanding the institutions of government for governance for the past fifty years. The expansion itself has created multi-faceted problems for the people by proliferating rules and regulations for people's activities. The loaded activities of the government through its institutions have pushed the people to the background. A perpetual gap has been developed and maintained between the people and the government. Government with its institutions with all weaknesses is able to maintain itself for the cause of the State and people who do not have much faith in it and continue to support the government as it provides space for their activities with freedom. Thus the whole issue of the society could be seen from this framework of State-dominated society for development.

Examination of Cases

Palatial buildings in the cities, towns and villages, proliferation of industries, expansion of communication system, spread of education at a massive scale through institutions, increasing market facilities, placement of variety of consumer goods in the market, sophistication in medical facilities, increasing banking activities by its quantum, multiplication of government institutions to look after the affairs of the people and increasing quantum of money available with the government have given an impression that the Indian society has achieved tremendously in many fronts. But a realistic and deep analysis of the issues of the people that the government is confronting would give a different picture which negates the path which we have trodden over the years to achieve development. Water and air— the entitlements of the people— now are polluted. The big government is not able to provide even the basic minimum facilities to the people. The minimum basic facilities like water supply, sanitation, medical facilities, educational opportunities, employment opportunities, common properties to support the life of the poor have not been properly provided to the public. It does not mean that the government has not made any effort in this regard. Government has taken steps to provide all these facilities to the people but they did not reach the people. In the meanwhile the development activities for economic growth have initiated consumeristic activities and utilised the natural resources at the maximum level and thereby the balance of the ecosystem has been disturbed. The government-initiated activities have distanced the people from the government. People did not know what policies are being pursued by the government and how they are to be used by the people. Government institutions have been multiplied and what for these institutions have been created is not known to the people. In the course of years the performance of the government provided enough scope for the officials to misuse the institutions at their discretion as the people are ignorant on many matters akin to government. Corruption became rampant everywhere. Problems in the society like insanitation, impure water, accumulation of dust on the streets, poor facilities in the schools, non-responsive officials in the government, poor facilities in the health centres, deforestation activities of the people in reserved forests and social forests, environmental degradation by the industries, air pollution by the transportation system, non-availability of employment opportunity, deteriorating law and order, erosion of ethical and moral values in private and public life and loss of family life due to individualistic style of functioning in the families have cautioned the State that the problems are beyond the level of the manageability of the governing institutions.[9] Crisis of governance is widely prevalent throughout the world as the rising expectations of the people from the government have increased beyond the capacity of the government. Most of the countries are performing both the tasks, namely, administering development and managing the crises simultaneously. But in India, crisis management takes away the major portion of time of the governing authorities and thus development administration takes place at a slow pace.

The mounting problems propelled the State authorities to think of an alternative. They suggest withdrawal of State from many areas of activities which were originally responsibilities of the communities. Reducing the structure of the government, leaving more responsibilities to the people's themselves is the major decision of the State in the present era.[10]

Insanitary conditions could be set right only by the people and not by the programmes of the government. Afforestation activities and arresting deforestation activities could be done only with the help of the communities. Environment of the society could be protected only by the people. Problems of the mass could be tackled by the people with the support of the government. Likewise for all issues people's cooperation is an imperative need.

The people's participation is very much invoked at present and is due to realising the mistake committed by the State in keeping the people away from the management of their own affairs in line with environmental conditions. People from the very beginning established a harmonious relationship with nature while exploiting the natural resources for their needs. But in order to fulfil the needs the State and the society have utilised the natural resources beyond the limits which has caused environmental degradation. The damages caused by the State and the society in environment have to be set right only by the involvement of the mass as a movement. State needs the active involvement of the people in the development process of the State.[11]

In India problems are always massive in nature. The massive problems could be tackled only by the involvement of the masses. To involve the masses an institutional mechanism is an imperative need. First a thorough analysis of the existing institutions is to be made. The relevance of the institutions in the context of their relationship with the society has to be seen. Secondly the role and reponsibilities have to be seen in the backdrop of the powers assigned to the institutions. Thirdly the possibility of handing over such role and responsibilities to the communities and withdrawing the institutions from their functioning has to be seriously viewed. While looking at all these issues primarily role and responsibilities have to be visualised from a basic framework of governance, namely, the governing institutions' structures. This can be done at three levels— at the district level, at the State level and at the level of the centre. Of the three structures, both at the centre and the State level institutions can be more formal and rigid as they are far away from the people and the district level institutions should have more flexibility and they should be informal and should be under the supervision of the people directly. In the same framework of governance, there is yet another possibility, namely, a two-tier structure of governance. They are federal government and district government and the State or provincial government could be eliminated if they are redundant.

Powers, role and responsibility could be visualised in terms of the stability of the State and the capacity of the society. Problems of the society and the State could be gauged from the bottom. They have to be classified in terms of the institutional mechanism required. Thus what could be done at lowest level or at the bottom could be left to the structure available at the grassroots level. What could not be done at the lowest level should be brought to the next level of institution and what could be done at this level could be allowed to be done at this level. What could not be achieved in the next level should be lifted to the third level of administration of development. What could be done at the third level should be allowed to be performed. What could not be done should be left to the next level. Likewise problems have to be tackled institution-wise depending upon the capacity of the institutions at different levels. By going through this process the present institutional structure and its corresponding power position would undergo a drastic change which ultimately would result in review of the Constitution of India. By doing so the unnecessary weight put on the federal government will be reduced. The community at the grassroots level will have more responsibilities and thereby unwanted government structure would be eliminated. Likewise the staff strength will be reduced. Correspondingly the complicated structures, rules, regulations, cumbersome procedures have to be eliminated. The above mentioned steps could be taken if there is political will or otherwise if there is any mass movement.[12] But conditions at present are so critical and hence the leaders at the helm of affairs have to think on this line as there is compulsion from various quarters. Moreover the government by its strength and weaknesses could not be able to perform its functions to the satisfaction of the people. This reform will bring closeness between the people and the government.

Inferences

The following are the inferences from the analysis of cases in Indian context from the backdrop of the framework which has been evolved:

1. Government is a source of trouble to the State and society.
2. Government structure has expanded to the maximum.
3. Staff strength has increased beyond the need of the government and the society.
4. There is a vast gap between the people and the government.
5. Rules, regulations norms and procedures are complicated and are not understandable to the public.
6. People have no responsibility.
7. There is no sense of community.
8. The present government has outlived the context.
9. Existing arrangement is prone to corruption.
10. People are far away from issues and problems.
11. The present arrangement has not improved the performance of the government.

Conclusion

The problems which we face in the society, namely, population explosion, illiteracy, unemployment, poor health, insanitary condition, environmental degradation, ethical crisis in public conduct have a direct bearing on the life of the people. These problems could be tackled only by the community and not through any institutional arrangement at the governmental level. Institutional mechanism could be evolved at the local level to involve the people in tackling the problem. Primarily steps have to be taken to create a sense of community among the people as they have lost that sense in the course of years due to the over-interference of the State in the community affairs.

Now there are models of participative governance. Kerala is setting an example even in the present archaic complicated structure. It is not a mere participation. It is contributory participative governance. There are communities in India taking care of themselves. At this juncture a new thinking is needed on the part of all to change the structure and style of governance and hence a marked departure is on the agenda of the society and government at present.

Notes and References

1. The change has been interpreted by Rajni Kothari in his article. For more details see Rajni Kothari, "Interpreting Indian Politics: A personal Statement" in *Crisis and Change in Contemporary India*, (eds), Upendra Baxi and Bikhu Parekh, New Delhi : Sage Publications, 1995 pp. 150-68.
2. Atul Kohli, "Crisis of Governability" in *Politics in India*, (ed.), Sudipta Kaviraj, Delhi: Oxford University Press, 1997.
3. Rajni Kothari, *State Against Democracy*, Delhi: Ajanta Publications, 1988.
4. Satish Saberwal, *India : The Roots of Crisis*, Delhi : Oxford University Press, 1986; Arun Bose, *India's Social Crisis*, Delhi Oxford University Press, 1985 and D.L. Seth "Social Basis of Political Crisis", *Seminar* (January, 1982).
5. For more details see James Manor, (ed.), *Rethinking Third World Politics*, London: Longman, 1991.
6. Rasheeduddin Khan, "The Total State : The Concepts and its Manifestation in the Indian Political System" in *The State Political Process and Identity : Reflections on Modern India*, New Delhi : Sage Publications, 1989.
7. For more details about the functions of the political system see David Easton, *The Political System*, Net York : Wiley & Sons, 1953; *A Framework for Political Analysis*, Englewood Cliffs NJ : Prentice Hall, 1965; *A System Analysis of Political Life*, New York: Wiley and Sons, 1965.

8. G.A. Almond and J.S. Coleman, *Politics of the Developing Areas*, Princeton : Princeton University Press, 1960.
9. M.F. Abraham, *The Agony of India*, Madras: East West Publishers, 1998.
10. Jayati Ghosh, "Development Strategy in India: A Political Economy Perspective" in *Nationalism, Democracy and Development: State and Politics in India*, (eds.) Sugata Bose and Ayesha Jalal, Delhi : Oxford University Press, 1998.
11. Kanchan Chopra, Gopal K. Kadekodi and M.N. Murty, *Participatory Development: People and Common Property Resources*, New Delhi : Sage Publications, 1990.
12. In this regard the Developing Countiries experiences have been explained in S.S. Meenakshisundaram, *Decentralization in Developing Countries*, New Delhi : Concept Publishing Company 1994.

6
Rural Reconstruction and Public Participation

Introduction

Even after fifty years of democratic governance in administering development, one cannot say that the villages are provided with adequate facilities to lead a decent human life. In many of the places, people are living in sub-human conditions. It does not mean that Government have not made efforts through policy options and resource allocation to ameliorate the conditions. Schemes and programmes for rural reconstruction were introduced even before the dawn of Independence.[1] Subsequently, government institutions have proliferated schemes and programmes from the period of community development to Integrated Rural Development Programme.[2] Despite all those schemes and programmes, Indian villages could not achieve development to lead a decent human life as envisaged. Questions have been raised periodically as to what contributes to the development of the society, whether capital, technology or government or manpower and so on.[3] Answers have been found out to the poor response of the schemes in the villages. Finally, the government have identified the answer: Development cannot be achieved in any society without the involvement of the people. How to involve the people in the development process is a major concern of the policy-makers of India today.[4]

The Problems and Perspectives

It is obvious that the concept of modern State system and

the western model of development have dominated the thought process of the policy-makers of India from the dawn of Independence.[5] Winning Independence is the first step in the development process of any society. Yet, while freeing the society, it has to choose its own model of development. The Indian National Congress after the entry of M.K. Gandhi changed its outlook as it was not merely to get freedom for India but also for reconstructing India. The conditions of the society warranted a perspective proposal to reconstruct the Indian society. M.K. Gandhi had developed a framework of human activities for the well-being of all.[6] Jawaharlal Nehru had a different framework of human activities for the same task of achieving well-being. The whole argument revolved around the State. Nehru had his own belief system that the emergence of modern nation-state and its impact could not be ignored and underestimated and hence nation-state by every sense has to play a dominant role in reconstructing the society. M.K. Gandhi who had a faith and conviction that any change could be brought about only by people's organisations through their involvement and participation. Any change could be effected only through the people by changing their mind-set. Imposition of any decision from the above cannot evoke any response unless it is accepted by the people. The newly formed State had usurped a number of responsibilities of the people. By doing so the people had been relegated to the background and the State is projected as pivotal and sole agency to bring development in the society. The problem here is : despite the concerted effort of the State through its policy options, programmes and schemes and with huge amount of resource allocation, development could not be achieved to the expectations of the people. Even the basic problems of the people have not been solved. What are the causes of this failure and what is the alternative to the existing arrangement[7] are some of the questions to be dealt with in this chapter.

Background

For any human activity whether it is individualistic or collective irrespective of its nature, a dominant thought process is essential. It had been the belief system of the people that all development efforts of the society could be undertaken only by the State. When integrating the collectivities to form a nation and to evolve a national identity, the State needed to assume powers and responsibilities. The problems of the people at that juncture had not been taken care of. They were very much in the items of the national agenda of the State. To tackle the problems of the people, the State apart from chalking out its plan of action, created a local structure to implement them.

Thus Panchayati Raj system was created throughout the country to implement the schemes and programmes of the government. Even at the dawn of Independence people's participation was ensured not in decision-making but in implementing the decisions of the government both at the federal and State levels.[8] Gradually government have expanded their activities as the quantum of the problems and their dimensions enlarged. Ministers have been increased and correspondingly government departments have been increased. As these institutions have been increased, activities have been expanded[9] and thereby every responsibility of the individual is taken away from them and vested in the government. Simultaneously political parties have increased their promises to the people with the belief that it is the responsibility of the government to provide all services to the people. People should be at the receiving end and government should be at the providing end.[10]

To retain the people under their fold, political parties have been competing with one another in giving assurances that more number of schemes and programmes would come from the government. This proliferation of schemes and programmes for development administered by the government not only relegated the people to the periphery but also helped the politicians and bureaucrats to misappropriate huge sums of money from these schemes and programmes and thus corrupt practices have been condoned as they are seen as a necessary evil to run the government machinery. All the ills that we witness today are due to concentration of powers at a centralised point. At a critical point, an alternative paradigm of development was conceived. In the new paradigm of development people's participation in the development process is an imperative. While examining the weaknesses in the development process, it is inferred that all necessary inputs have been provided for development as in the western countries by adopting the western model excepting the people's involvement and hence results could not be achieved as intended by the government. But the problems in the society are so critical in the rural areas. Now the rural areas are to be reconstructed. How they should be reconstructed is a major question.[11]

Rural Realities

People are not living in peace. Communities are quarrelling with each other in sharing resources and in breaking the established social order. The common properties which have provided opportunities to the poor to sustain their life have been taken over by politically and socially influential individuals and groups with the support of the administration. The total support base of the poor has been eroded by the intervention of the State. Modernization and westernization have influenced the life-style of the people by and large and it resulted in keeping them aloof from the responsibilities to be discharged as community and moreover the cleanliness of the villages has been a neglected aspect in rural life. Equally industrialization has polluted the rural areas through its activities. Water has been polluted everywhere. The free supply of electricity to farmers has drained the underground water and as a result non-availability of drinking water to the poor without the help of the government is a problem. Villages are in the trap of insanitation. Children in the families of the poor are not brought up in such a manner as they ought to be brought up. Facilities which have been created in the health sector to meet the requirements of the people in the rural areas have not reached the rural poor. Officials who are working in the rural development sectors are not responsive to the needs of the people. They are not only non-responsive but they are also oppressive by way of exploiting them for the services done to them. The traditionally developed skills of the rural masses have not been used for productive purposes. Agriculture has become a cultural activity rather than a commercial and profitable enterprise. Day by day farmers are being marginalised. Uneducated youth and educated youth without having employment opportunity while away their time in the public places and sometimes they indulge in anti-social activities. Rural women continue to parade in the evening and morning on the road or on the outskirts for want of toilet facilities. Thus problems are multiplied and expectations of the people have increased due to the change in the life-style of the people and thereby the structure of the government has been broad-based. The total State system has tolerated the mind-set of the people, bureaucrats and politicians.[12] The failures of the State have been accepted by the authorities of the government. In the process of identifying an alternative to the existing pattern of development, the State itself found out a solution called "Empowerment of the people".

Empowering People

Empowering people for what? is the question to be answered here. State-building or nation-building was so popular among the people in the 40s and 50s. Equally province-building was so popular among the people during the 60s and 70s. Empowerment of people refers to the conferment of power and authority on the people to look after some of the affairs of the people in a given geographical area. It further refers to giving authority not to the representatives of the people in the institutions but to people themselves as community. Thus the intention is to entrust the responsibilities to the community which are taken from the State. This empowerment is meant for altering the mind-set of the people to look at the government as not a provider but a facilitator and to look at themselves not as receivers of benefits but stake-holders in the development process as participants. The participation of the people does not start with implementation stage, it will begin with decision-making itself.

Reconstruction by Participation

The whole process of empowering people has taken shape through an amendment to the Constitution of India and thus a permanent institutional mechanism was evolved to make the people participate in the development process. A point here has to be clarified unequivocally as to whether the institutional mechanism evolved to make the people participate in the development is in line with the centralised pattern of development through decentralised operation of schemes and programmes for poverty eradication, growth and development. It is a general belief among the major sections of the politicians, administrators, local leaders and people that the local institutions created through the 73rd amendment to the Constitution of India are to implement the schemes and programmes of the federal and State governments with the amount provided by those governments. "Local bodies are the agencies which have got only agency functions" is the belief of the majority in the society. But, in reality, it is not so. It is an institution, constitutionally recognised with earmarked powers and responsibilities to involve the people in the development process. It is for economic development and social justice. It has to chalk out schemes and programmes to meet not only the basic needs but also for economic development. It should not rely on the resources from the above (i.e., the State and the Centre). This is an institution with more flexibility instead of regidity as one has witnessed in the activities of the Centre and State governments even though it is more or less like a government. The State and Central governments are being operated through a representative body but the grassroots institution has to be operated only by the people.[13]

The problems which we face in the rural areas do not need huge amount of money but the involvement of the people with a commitment to solve the problems. Sanitation is a problem in the rural areas. This problem cannot be solved with the programmes and schemes of the government. It can be solved only by the people. Disposal of nightsoil with the available technology can also solve the problem. It is very difficult to provide western type of toilet facilities to all houses throughout the country and hence to dispose of the night-soil, a simple device which is acceptable to their mode of life is to be evolved with the approval of the people by which every street and every village is free from the menace of the night-soil and for which no grand scheme is needed from the above as the centralised schemes have already failed miserably. It is more important that to what extent it is profitable to every individual should be demonstrated to the people. When it is practised in many places at the micro level and the success is demonstrated, no wonder every village will follow suit. Thus the fertility of the soil will be increased and cleanliness will be ensured.

Yet another menace is the waste deposited on road sides without dumping it in the pit for compost manure. The waste cannot be used as it is for compost making as nonbiodegradable materials have been mixed in all the waste. In most of the villages the carry-bags made of polythene material get mixed into the dust which prevents the waste to become compost manure. A new culture has to be developed among the people to classify the waste and biodegradable waste has to be put in a compost pit to convert it into an organic manure. By doing this, primarily villages will be clean, neat and profit could be gained by the owners of the pit and more particularly unutilised energy will be used. Disposal of night-soil and waste is not a simple thing at this juncture as the mind-set is different but it requires only the will-power and not money. Now it is the reponsibility of the people to take care of this problem and for this issue the village community has to initiate action plans.

Common properties traditionally have provided life opportunity to the poor and now it is gradually degraded and shared among the politically and socially influential groups. The common properties such as grazing ground, different kinds of porompokku, roads, trees on the roads, tanks, wells, lakes, market places and buildings are not properly maintained as a result they are not yielding expected resources to the common good fund. Wherever people's organisations are maintaining them, they are in good condition but they are in the user's control and hence they are not adequately useful to the poor. To perform the entrusted responsibilities, needed resources could be obtained from the commons by the participation of the people in the maintenance, protection and enrichment of commons.[14] Commons have to be retrieved from illegal holdings by the joint venture of the people, they have to be enriched and they are to be properly managed so as to bring huge amount of resources to the community action. Commons help the poor and the marginalised. By enriching the commons, environment will be protected and it would generate more economic activities. It would generate more employment opportunities for the poor and the skilled persons.

Further, the facilities such as health and primary education are vital for human resource development. What we face at the higher level education (poor standard) is the offshoot of weak foundation at primary level education and likewise the poor health of the people is due to non-responsive functioning of the health sector. If the two institutions perform their task on the expected lines our development would be much more higher than what we have. Primary education is left to the discretion of the government manned by the officials which have no connection with the local people and environment and as a result it has come to a sorry state of affairs. People who have aspirations have invested hard-earned money apart from paying for education with the government through their taxes by sending their wards to private educational institutions. People who have no other option have been sending their wards to government schools. Now these schools are under the purview of the local bodies.

The primary schools need only the attention of the people not the money as it is being enhanced to equip the rural schools by providing more facilities. Surroundings of the schools have to be clean and it should be maintained with hygiene and high sanitary conditions. It is to be checked whether the provided facilities are intact and are in full use. It should be ensured that all the teachers of the schools are punctual, regular, attentive, work-oriented and value-based. By a constant interaction between the community and the teachers, conditions of the schools would be improved. The improved atmosphere would attract the attention of the people and more number of students would turn towards the rural schools.

Likewise the health sector which is essential for the community, is in disarray. People's faith in government health institutions has faded away as the services of the health centres created by the government are poor. The mushroom growth of private institutions thrives only on the failure of the government sector. For the rich it is not a problem but to the poor it is very difficult to manage money for the health expenditure.

By the intervention of the people, the existing maladies in the health sector could be eliminated. Personnel will be attentive, responsive and service-oriented if the people are vigilant and active in supervising the institutions. If facilities are not adequate they can also be provided by proper representation to local bodies and to local M.L.A. By making this earnest effort, natal care, post-natal care, child development, reproductive health care, women development and preventing epidemics could be adequately attended to and human resource could be developed on par with other developed countries. Investment on health through the budget is not very low but the proper utilisation of the amount for the said purposes is very minimum. Hence what we need is the participation of the people as community to supervise the health sector in appropriate form as per the provision available in the amendment.

Yet another area providing employment to the poor in the rural areas, is a vital issue to be tackled. Is it so easy ? It is very difficult as the skills available in the rural areas are not capable to produce marketable goods. And even if the available skills are used to produce articles, it is very difficult to find market for these products. So the skilled person's capacity has to be enhanced to produce marketable products. By gauging the trend in the development process, identify the areas of employment potential and plan for production units to produce articles which are in great demand and for which traditional science, traditional technology and traditional machines will be of immense use.

Herbal products alone will give employment opportunity for millions from growing medicinal plants to producing medicine. Handicraft is yet another area for concentration to generate employment opportunity. Mass of the articles have to be produced and emporiums have to be started in all the towns to sell these commodities. Just like F.D. Roosevelt's policy, all types of works can be done in the rural areas in small units and a network of production and marketing has to be created with the help of the State and Central governments.

People have to understand the primary functions of all development departments and watch over the performance of all these departments. By doing a watchdog function, many of the offices could be brought under social audit system. If there is any resistance, people have to be organised against such corrupt and negligent officials. While taking up many responsibilities by the people, a sizable reduction of government departments is imperative and imminent.

Conclusion

The State has lost its relevance in performing the development functions any more. It can maintain unity and at the most law and order. We see the crisis in governance. Devolving powers to the people to take up responsibility would enable local institutions to have control over the departments of the government. Local body institutions should not function as a representative body but they should be the people's organisations. They should be more flexible than the State and Central governments. The real issues which are affecting the life of the people in the rural areas need no money but a change of mind-set and involvement of the people. All service facilities could be managed by the people and development activities could also be designed, schemes and programmes could also be evolved by the people themselves. Hence to reconstruct the Indian rural society, an institution to respond and to care to the needs of the people has come to stay. It is the institution of the people which will function under the control of the people.

It is not a scheme and it is a movement of the people to achieve growth and equity. Social justice could be effectively brought about by the local institution with the approval of the Gram Sabha.

Notes and References

1. S.R. Maheswari, *Rural Development in India*, New Delhi: Sage Publications, 1985, pp. 22-35.
2. Ministry of Rural Areas and Employment, *Programmes for Change*, New Delhi: Ministry of Rural Areas and Employment, 1997.
3. Garry Jacobs, *Development Education: An Introductory Explanation*, Pondicherry: The Mother's Service Society, 1982, pp. 6-8.
4. Hari Mohan Mathur, *Administering Development in the Third World*, New Delhi: Sage Publications, 1986, pp. 13-51.
5. Bhikhu Parekh, "Jawaharlal Nehru and the crisis of Modernization" in *Crisis and Change in Contemporary India* (eds.) Upendra Baxi and Bhikhuel Parekh, New Delhi : Sage Publications, 1995, pp. 21-56.
6. Anthony J. Parel, "The Doctrine of Swaraj in Gandhi's Philosophy" in *Crisis and Change in Contemporary India* (ed.) *ibid.* pp. 57-81.
7. Sudipta Kaviraj, "On State, Society and Discourse in India" in *Rethinking Third World Politics*, (ed.) James Manor, London : Longman 1991, pp. 72-99.
8. George Mathew, *New Panchayati Raj System : From Legislation to Movement*, New Delhi : Concept Publications, 1996.
9. By careful analysis and comparison of the departments of governments over a period of time, one would find the bigness of the government. It is not peculiar to India alone. It is a universal phenomenon. For details, see Daniel J. Elazar, "Opening the Third Century of American Federalism : Issues and Prospects" *The Annals of the American Academy of Political and Social Science* (May 1990), pp. 11-21.
10. Totally a dependency syndrome has been developed among the people and this syndrome is afflicting the society as a disease. To remove this syndrome handing over responsibilities to the people through an organised way is the only solution available with the State. New Panchayati Raj System is one among such measures. For more details, see G. Palanithurai (ed.), *Empowering People : Issues and Solutions*, New Delhi : Kanishka Publications, 1997.

11. S. Narayansamy, "Constructive Programme towards the Twenty-first Century" *Gandhi Marg* (Oct.-Dec. 1997), pp. 341-51.
12. S.C. Dube, *Understanding Change : Anthropological and Sociological Perspectives*, New Delhi : Vikas Publishing House Pvt. Ltd., 1992.
13. Rajiv Gandhi Foundation, *Proceedings of National Workshop on Panchayati Raj*, New Delhi : RGF, 1993.
14. Kanchan Chopra, Gopal K. Kadekodi and M.N. Murty, *Participatory Development : People and Common Property Resources*, New Delhi : Sage Publications, 1990.

7
A Framework for Reconstruction of Villages

Introduction

Villages of today will not reflect the characteristics of the villages of yester day, yester year and yester decade. The continuous accelerated activities of the State, by the economic vision of the leaders and planners to achieve economic development, have directed the society to move in a direction which has been shown by the westerners.[1] The society which had its own path of progress has lost its track and moved in different directions by changing the belief system, values, attitudes, institutions, behaviour and performance of the individuals and groups. The initiated activities were intended to remove the age old ills and to equalise the communities and sections in terms of the facilities and services.[2] But in reality, instead of removing the ills, the State activities have increased the ills as the activities of the State have not been properly perceived. The gradual increase in State activities made the people to depend on it for many things and especially for services in the name of welfare. Villages which had been in the grip of poverty and social ills due to the social structure had been visualised very seriously by the planners and leaders of the country. But the ills and maladies which we are witnessing are much more serious than the maladies of the society in the previous era. The malaise at present is due to the inflow of information related to development through the communication network developed by the State system. Hence villages of today have plethora of problems which are very serious in nature.[3] Unless these problems are solved, there won't be any future for the rural areas in India.

The Problems

Problems in the rural areas vary from area to area. Regional disparities are obvious and they are bound to exist in a country like India as perceptions and performance of individuals vary due to the varying capacity of individuals. Even after fifty years of Independence through democratic governance, India is not able to make a proclamation that it provides conditions to the people to lead a good human life. People live in sub-human conditions in many parts of the country. People are discriminated over caste and class.[4] Escalating violence took the life of many. People are struggling to get their entitlements. Expanded government machineries have started terrorising the people and people are made to fall in the trap of corruption and thereby corruption has been accepted as an institution to accelerate the speed of activities of the individuals and institutions.[5] Population explosion coupled with increasing illiteracy has threatened the State authorities that the vitals of the society for economic growth are at stake.[6] Proliferation of private institutionalised service facilities has attracted the rustic folk. The service institutions like hospitals, primary health centres, primary schools, cooperative societies, agricultural institutions created by the government, have been made to distance themselves from the hold of the people and their organisations due to the organised effort of the staff who work in these institutions. The deterioration of these institutions has made the people to rely on private institutions. The continuous accelerated activities of the State, State-oriented elites, business groups have completely subjected the government to succumb to the pressure and sometimes government institutions are subordinated. In the process of accelerated economic activities have spoiled the environment, utilised the natural resource excessively and as a result rural areas have been drained resource-wise and natural green cover has been removed. Technology and its application making articles for markets have driven the artisans and skilled labourers in various trades in the rural areas out of job and they have been made jobless and under-utilised. Thus the villages are made as centres of non-economic activities, non-profit agricultural activities and unskilled labourers.[7] The new image of life created by the media from the perspective of modernization and westernization has shaken the foundation of values of community life and family life. We find only individuals and not families and communities. Thus State-proliferated problems are more in number and their intensity is much more complicated. To solve all these issues and problems a series of steps have to be taken.

A Framework for Rural Reconstruction

We are in the fifth development decade and witnessing tumultuous changes in the State and society in terms of the development process. Developed countries have witnessed fast changes and thereby the exponents of development noticed the instability and uncertainty of the development achieved over the past. Time has come to talk about sustainability of development or sustainable development. The westerners' notion of development always refers to the economic growth. So far the economic growth conceptualised by the exponents of development in the West has not found out a base for sustainability and hence criticisms have been attributed towards the theories on economic growth enunciated by the western scholars. For the sustainability of growth the activities of humanity towards the economy should have some basic unalterable principles in an oceanic circle. The very basic principle is the harmony between the nature and the human actions. What we find in the market economy is nothing but products or articles made out of natural resources. The accelerated speed of economic activities has increased the exploitation of natural resources. The excess exploitation of natural resources brought an imbalance in the order of cosmos. What all we see today in the form of degradation of nature is due to the over-exploitation of natural resources by man to make products or articles for economic growth. To make the people to consume the products and articles people's consumeristic attitude has been developed by the media through advertisement. In the entire process of the accelerated economic activities, the senses have been tuned to consume more and more for pleasure. Seeking pleasure has been made the central objective of the human activities today that deprives the millions even to have the basic minimum for a decent human living. The world's most worrisome problem of conflict starts only with sharing the pleasures and the pains of humanity. This uncertainty and inhuman tendency should not and cannot continue in the future as people are becoming aware of what is going on in the society. As long as the people feel that the State will ensure parity in distribution among the collectivities and individuals, people will exhibit restrain and the moment the people feel that the State is not for the poor, disorderliness will creep into the system. The world is witnessing paradoxical situation today. Economic growth is being achieved by societies, population is fast increasing, disparity between the rich and the poor continues to increase, conflict among the collectivities to share the growth has also increased. This state of affairs indicates that the fault lies in the system.

Today's conditions warrant a thorough analysis of the institutions, organisations and society's behaviours and performances over the years.[8] What all the changes we have been seeing the society, polity and economy cannot be termed as negative and not conducive for the betterment of the society and equally they cannot be termed as positive and conducive for the betterment of the society. It is a mixture of both positive and negative. Arguments are for both. Terming the nature of the change depends on one's own perception about development. Because the theories which have been developed on development over the years have not explained the aspects uniformly and most of the occasions one would find more in congruent arguments. So far there has been no final agreement over the concept.[9] In the meanwhile the concept has been fragmented into divisions, namely political development, social development, economic development and cultural development. The basic question is whether these developments address the basic issues of the society today.

In the political front, elections are being conducted periodically. It does not mean that the society has achieved political development. The quality of democracy determines the level of political development. Social structures are being weakened and it does not mean the society has achieved social development. There have been changes in the society but it does not mean that they all lead to betterment. Likewise changes have taken place in the sub-systems of the larger social systems. Yet these changes have escalated more and more problems in the society rather than solving the social, economic and political problems. First one should list out the problems and find out the solutions to those problems.

Even after fifty years of Independence, we are not in a position to create awareness among the people about election and its implications. Without knowing the system, people have cast their votes in all the twelve general elections. As a result our political system is in the hands of self-centred, short-sighted and unwilled politicians. People do not know how to choose a right person to representative institutions. So everybody feels that there is a perception gap between the people and the politicians about our political system. The unwanted men and women have entered politics and the wise have joined the ranks of bureaucracy. Yet another section of the community pursued their own branch of work, namely, business. The people who have high esteem for their own profession agriculture continue to perform agricultural operations. The mass on the whole who have been oriented to follow the dictum of the State continue to follow the dictates of the State. The people who are becoming aware of the state of affairs today try to express their voice strongly against the State. The dissent voice has being growing against the State despite the steps taken by the State for all round development of the society during the past fifty years. Where have the fruits of development gone and who have been benefited by the schemes and programmes is a major question. It is obvious that it was felt that people do not know much about the democracy that we have today and the administrative mechanism since people are far away from the political and administrative system. People who know the working of this complicated system have exploited the same for their own advantage. To avoid or to eliminate this either the people's capacity has to be increased or the ruling structure has to be so simplified that the people can understand the same. As long as the user understands the utility of the product, he will be more alert so as to oversee the system which produces the product. Hence a governing system which is understandable to the people could be created.[10]

The economy is yet another important aspect which has complicated the human life. Economic activities in any society should be need-based and not greed-based.[11] The third world countries are still struggling to provide basic minimum facilities to the people for a decent human living. The western countries are engaged in adding to the comforts of the people at the cost of the resources of many generations. Their path of progress is only to enhance luxuries of life. In our country we are also following the same path to achieve parity with them. By following the western path of prosperity, we have also sharpened the taste for enjoying pleasure at the cost of resources instead of achieving equity. There is a major difference between the West and the East especially in items of resource exploitation. Western countries have exploited the resources of other countries by keeping their natural resources in reserve. In India we are exploiting the natural resources for our own use and for other societies. We cannot and should not use the resources as the western societies have done, because our population is vast and to meet their expanding needs we have to exhaust resource very fast. Resource conservation is the primary task of the society in India today.

To perform this new task the age-old institutions have to be revived. It does not mean the age-old social institutions. It is only revival of mechanics adopted by the ancient institutions as they were catering only to the needs of the people and not to the greed of them. Further the people are to be made conscious of the organic relationship between the nature and the human beings. Scientific devices and technological innovations have to be used appropriately. Political and economic institutions have to be so devised that the people can understand them. People's capacity has to be increased to make use of the institutions. To perform the above-mentioned tasks, modifications in the existing arrangement or reforming the institutional structure will not help. The entire process of transformation has to begin with the change of mind-set. The change of mind-set has to begin with the leaders who are able to control the mass. Thus the need of the hour is a movement of the masses, not a committee of experts or intellectuals.

Analysing the Indian Situations

The whole of Indian society, polity and economy could be visualised from two main perspectives, namely, poverty and prosperity. There are portrayals about the success stories of India through democratic governance in the past fifty years. Establishment of institutions, namely, government, industrial, educational and political and their implications on the society have been projected as positive achievements of the Indian society. The increasing cry for basic facilities such as water, employment opportunities, medical facilities, educational facilities, proper distribution of essential commodities for the people through public distribution system, providing basic infrastructural facilities has sounded the alarm to the State that it has failed in meeting these entitlements of the people. The Indian State is so soft but it does not mean it is insensitive. It has been vigilant and active in many fronts, that is why it is able to withstand all frontal attacks of human collectivities. Even the integration of Indian nation has been questioned by many intellectuals in the past fifty years. The exponents of nationalism and State have predicted that the integration of Indian communities into an Indian nation has always been a problem. The Indian State has got a resilience of tackling the crises. It has been reflected in the past few years when weak leaders assumed higher responsibilities of governance. The questions such as "After Nehru who? "After Indira who? "Crises in governability" "Stress and strain in Indian State" have been well-answered through the governing process of the country in the past few years.[12]

The concepts like developmentalism initiated by Nehru, eradication of poverty initiated by Indira Gandhi and taking India to the twenty-first century by Rajiv Gandhi through new policy options have attracted the communities and drawn them towards the State. The developmentalism of Nehru and poverty eradication movement of Indira Gandhi had mostly relied on the State action from initiation to implementation. But Rajiv Gandhi's new approach of taking India to 21st century is fully based on the initiation of the people. The State has a minimum role and people have a greater role in the development process of the society. This new line of thinking in the Indian setting has its own roots in the changes of the global environment. This new venture needs marathon exercises to build the capacity of the people, bureaucracy and politicians. Problems at the lowest level are immense and to tackle the same many capacitated individuals are needed everywhere. The problems that we face in the villages are complicated as they are caught in the web of modernization and particularly the consumeristic culture. From food habit to dressing pattern radical changes have been witnessed during the past fifty years. In the name of economic growth. exploitation of the natural resources at a higher speed has been encouraged. Purposely, the consumeristic trend has been encouraged and as a result the concept of saving has been given a go by.

To redeem the situation the mind-set of the people has to be changed. The systems which had been introduced by the British in polity, economy, science and technology have to be contextually thought of and it is high time to review and retrace the original polity, economy science and technology which the Indian communities practised for centuries. Traditional polity was understandable to the people, economy was known to the people, science technology and medicine had been evolved by the communities over the years till the advent of the British and hence people had a grip over polity, economy, science, technology and medicine. Now the human collectivities have to move from the present modern life-style to ecofriendly, nature-prone, community-based activities.

It is not so easy to bring back the people from the mad consumeristic culture to ecodevelopment culture because consumeristic culture provides pleasure to senses. Seeking sensory pleasure is the nucleus of life in the society. The people have been oriented to this culture. To bring back the people from the modern trend of seeking pleasure to satisfying the basic minimum needs of the individual and collectivity, a series of steps have to be taken.

How can we inject this thought in the minds of the people is a daunting question. At present the whole of urban people have been fully oriented to the lifestyle suited to western culture. But eighty per cent of the people in the rural areas are struggling where to go and how to go? But the undecided lot have also been oriented indirectly towards modern life yet they have nothing to sustain it as their economy does not permit them to lead that life-style and as a result all corrupt and anti-social activities crept in to the social milieu. If anyone were convincingly to inform the people in the rural areas that the life pattern which they lead at present is harmful to nature, the people will not fall a prey to this new life pattern. If people are not adhering to this way of life, it is entirely due to ineffective way of communicating these ideas to the people.

The modern life pattern has created more problems in the society in terms of sanitation, water supply and health. The rich have resources to protect themselves from the problems generated by the consumeristic culture. The poor are the victims. To keep the environment clean and healthy, instead of relying on the government, the community has to do it on its own. To discharge the responsibilities entrusted to them they need to have an institutional mechanism. Apart from this, for all community activities, people need technology known to them. So science and technology have to be developed and the efforts in this direction are to be supported by the government.

Conclusion

The present trend of growth and development has to be seen

in the context of the transformation that takes place in the rural areas. The depletion of natural resources, pollution of natural resources, exploitative culture, consumeristic culture, intense social tension and conflict, conflicting cultural values have altered the mind-set of the people. The present trend cannot continue forever. Unless it is stopped, rural areas will become deserts and seed-bed for all types of conflicts and confrontations. To achieve ecofriendly life-style and to achieve sustainable development a new mind-set has to be created. Science and technology which are known to the people have to be developed. Institutional mechanisms which are familiar to the people have to be developed. A new leadership has to be developed in the rural areas which will be able to mobilise the people and make the people to participate in the development process. Thus a new life pattern has to be developed where all positive aspects of modern life and culture could be taken up and fused together to create a new framework for achieving nature-based sustainable development.

Notes and References

1. Pranab Bardhan, "The State Against Society: The Great Divide in Indian Social Science Discourse" in *Nationalism, Democracy and Development,* (eds), Sugata Bose and Ayesha Jalal, Delhi: Oxford University Press, 1997, p. 186.
2. B.C. Mathur "Emerging Issues in Public Administration" *Indian Institute of Public Administration Souvenir 1998.*
3. Paul McCarthy, *Post-modern Desire Learning from India*, New Delhi : Promilla & Co. Publishers, 1994.
4. Dipankar Gupta, "Continuous Hierarchies and Discrete Castes, "*Social Stratification*, Delhi : Oxford University Press, 1997.
5. Values have been changed frequently and hence there is no stiff resistance from the masses to arrest the corrupt practices perpetuated by the politicians, bureaucrats both jointly and individually.
6. Population Foundation of India, *State of India's Population*, New Delhi : PFI Publications, 1998.
7. For the existing problems in the rural areas, solutions have been extensively discussed in V. Padmanabhan, *A Grammar for Rural Development*, Madurai : Khadi Friends Forum, 1996.

8. Excellent analysis has been made in the report of a commission and for more details see International Commission on Peace and Food, *Uncommon Opportunities : An Agenda for Peace and Equitable Development*, London : Zed Books, 1994.
9. For a detailed analysis, see Mother's Service Society, *Development Education : An Introductory Explanation*, Pondicherry : The Mother's Service Society, 1982.
10. A framework could be evolved on the basis of the perception of M.K. Gandhi on political system. One should give much thought to his Gram Swaraj. M.K. Gandhi, *Village Swaraj*, Ahmedabad : Navajivan Publishing House, 1962.
11. A new economic perspective could be developed from the framework of J.C. Kumarappa. For more details, see J.C. Kumarappa, *Economy of Permanence*, Varanasi : Sarva Seva Sangh Prakashan, 1962.
12. For more details, see G. Palanithurai, *Indian Polity : Myth and Reality*, New Delhi : Kanishka Publishers & Distributors, 1993.

8

Struggling Grassroots Democracy in Indian Society

Introduction

73rd and 74th Amendments to the Constitution of India made the functioning of local body institutions mandatory to achieve economic development and social justice. To perform this task a guided structural framework has been given to all State governments. The State governments have to go about it through the framework to activate the local body institutions. From the enactment of the law, we have seen the activities of the local bodies in various provinces for the past five years. The grass-roots institutions are in different stages of execution of the programmes. Efforts are on to evaluate the functioning of the local body institutions to find out emerging pattern and to indicate the drawbacks both in the structure and functioning of the institutions. The federal and State governments are to take appropriate steps to correct the defective mechanism and functioning of the grassroots institutions.[1]

The Problem

Success of any scheme or programme depends on a number of factors such as how best the schemes are operationally conceived, how best the schemes are perceived by the personnel who implement them and how best the beneficiaries understood the scheme or programme?[2] No doubt, the New Panchayati Raj System is not a scheme or a programme, it is a mass movement by itself.[3] Yet the New Panchayati Raj System is perceived as a new programme by many as it has been introduced through a central legislation. India, being a multi-ethnic society with varying geographical climate, diverse socio-economic conditions and with huge population, may not be able to execute any scheme as successfully as is being done in the western society. From perception to performance one would find a significant difference in the Indian masses due to variation in the capacity of the people at different levels.

A Framework for Analysis[4]

New Panchayati Raj has been conceptualised differently. There are different schools of thought which interpret and explain the new system of governance differently. Those who look at the new Panchayati Raj System through historical approach try to explain the new arrangement as an extension of the old system with additional responsibilities. Looking at the phenomenon from the historical perspective would no doubt enlighten our knowledge of its understanding. But it has to be analysed and explained contextually. There is yet another school trying to explain from the Gandhian framework of Gram Swaraj which is totally contradictory in nature. Gandhi's Gram Swaraj cannot be seen through this new dispensation of empowerment. Yet they try to look at it from the point of view of Gram Swaraj.

The third school which has its base on Nehru's Panchayati Raj which has to visualise the whole arrangement as an instrument to carry out the governments programmes and schemes. Most of the bureaucrats belong to this school. Pointing out the weak capacity of these institutions and their managerial ability, these institutions can only act as an instrument to carry out programmes and schemes.

The fourth school of thought brings an argument from the western perspective of the civil society which is basically a liberation movement liberating the people from the clutches of the total State system. The argument stems from the fact that the evolution of the new system is to bring an alternative approach to achieve growth and development on a sustainable basis with equity and social justice. This has been the projection of the NGO and intellectual sectors.

Another school is purely an economic orientation which conceptualises the new system of arrangement in the context of liberalization and globalization with the aim of bringing more number of collectivities under the influence of the market economy. It is mere expansion of market-oriented economy. The New liberal school has been consistently advocating its economic implications.

Sixth school of thought looks at the whole scheme of things from the framework of Rajiv Gandhi, who was instrumental in making a series of exercises to find out a viable alternative system of governance to achieve economic development and social justice and who piloted the historic 64th Amendment Bill in parliament and met with a failure. He envisaged a new framework of policy options with an objective of taking India to the 21st century to compete with other societies who are far ahead of India in terms of socio-economic growth.

Operationalisation of the New Arrangement

All the schools have got their strong bases to develop approaches to explain, visualise and analyse the functioning of the new system of governance. Contextually everyone is deviating from the reality as 73rd and 74th constitutional amendments are a compromise formula between supporters and detractors of the new dispensation as envisaged by Rajiv Gandhi. Rajiv Gandhi's dispensation is deviant from Gram Swaraj for self sufficiency and reliance and Nehruvian Panchayati Raj for raising infrastructure to implement schemes and programmes, even though some of the basic elements of Gram Swaraj and Nehruvian Panchayati Raj are in it. Civil society approach tends to claim this from the 11th schedule of works to be assigned to people's organisation with much emphasis on the power of the people through Gram Sabha. They emphasise the participation of the people in the development process. Hence it cannot be a Panchayati Raj with traditional outlook as portrayed with prejudice by Dr. B.R. Ambedkar and likewise it cannot be as Gram Swaraj conceptualised by M.K. Gandhi.

It can be neither a civil society nor a Panchayati Raj of Nehruvian model of an implementing agency. It can be a new structural arrangement as visioned by Rajiv Gandhi since the contentious issues and areas have been eliminated from the Bill introduced as 72nd Amendment Bill and passed as 73rd Constitutional Amendment Act. Hence operational dimension could be seen only from 73rd Constitutional Amendment as it gives legal sanction and it is being operationalised in the provinces through the guidance of the Ministry of Rural Areas and Employment. The new operational framework should have the following key characteristics :

1. It is a constitutional entity;
2. It has the characteristics of a government except law making;
3. It has got a three-tier system;
4. Gram Sabha is the basic unit of the system for people's participation;
5. District Planning Committe is the constitutionally regionalised unit for micro level planning;
6. State Finance Commission to suggest modalities to share resources between the State and the Panchayats;
7. One-third reservation of seats in all positions in all the three tiers for women;
8. Reservation of seats in all positions in all the three tiers for SC/ST proportionate to their population;
9. Allocation of 29 subjects in the 11th Schedule to panchayats;
10. Constituting an Election Commission to conduct the election periodically;
11. Election to Panchayati bodies every five years is mandatory.

Keeping all these characteristics as basis for the New Panchayati Raj system one has to evaluate the functioning of the panchayats at all levels in all the States of India. While evaluating the functioning and performance, the governing clause of the 73rd Constitutional Amendment 243 (G) has to be taken into account. 243 (G) states that economic development and social justice are the twin objectives of the new Panchayati Raj system.[5]

To operate the new system every State has to amend the existing Act or to enact a new Act. The act has to reflect the spirit of the 73rd Constitutional Amendment Act.

Before taking stock of the situation, we have to analyse the perception of the people who involve themselves in the implementation process of the New Panchayati Raj System. When 64th Amendment Bill was introduced in the Parliament, a series of articles have been written and letters have been written to the Prime Minister by the provincial leaders and leaders of some national political parties in this regard. The letters and articles reflect the mood of the leaders of the provinces and intellectuals. Their basic argument is that the State has been bypassed. Their contention is that power has to be devolved only through the State government and with this perception, implementation process has to be assessed. The implementation of the new system depends on the perception of the leaders of the State government, bureaucracy, intellectuals, leaders of local body institutions and the people.[6]

A Case Analysis of Tamil Nadu

In Tamil Nadu the DMK and the AIADMK are claiming that they are the champions of State autonomy and more powers to the State and have raised opposition both to 64th and 73rd Amendment to the Constitution of India. Even for the defeat of the 64th Amendment Bill a member of the AIADMK in Rajya Sabha contributed by absenting himself from voting.

The credit of vociferous opposition to decentralization of power goes to these Dravidian parties. After the enactment of the 73rd Amendment Act the then ruling party in Tamil Nadu the AIADMK slept over it for an year. At the fag end, it took up the matter to fulfil the constitutional obligation and passed a new Local Bodies Act in 1994.[7] Without much discussion on the Bill in the Assembly it was passed in the absence of the opposition party. By doing this the AIADMK has discredited itself by bringing one of the most backward Acts in India with regard to the empowerment of the people.[8] The Act has been enacted but there was no action for the conduct of election. They found out the way to escape from the act of conducting election to local bodies. An ordinance was issued to provide reservation of seats for backward class in local bodies and this instrument has been used to stop the election through the court intervention.

First we will take up the Act for examination. What are the characteristics of the new provincial Act. The key features of the 73rd Constitutional Amendment have to be accommodated otherwise it will be construed as violative of the constitutional provision. The Tamil Nadu Panchayati Act has been enacted in 1994 in such a fashion as to accommodate the key characteristics of the 73rd Constitutional Amendment Act only in form and not in spirit. The salient features of the new Act are as follows :

(a) a three-tier system;
(b) Gram Sabha;
(c) Establishment of Election Commission;
(d) Constitution of Finance Commission;
(e) Reservation of seats for SC/ST proportionate to their population;
(f) One-third reservation of seats for women; and
(g) Constitution of District Planning Committee.

Gram Sabha

Gram Sabha is the nucleus of the New Panchayati Raj System. All the registered voters are members of the Gram Sabha of that Village Panchayat. It has to meet thrice a year and at least once in six months. President of Gram Panchayat is the presiding officer of the meetings of Gram Sabha. Gram Sabha has to give approval to the budget proposal and annual plan of the village panchayat. Further it has to give approval to the annual audited statement on the expenditure of the village panchayat. One-tenth forms the quorum to transact the business of the Gram Sabha. In Tamil Nadu, Gram Sabha is a neglected subject and unit in the local body arrangement as both elected leaders and officials have not shown any interest in it due to many reasons. As per the Government orders, even beneficiaries for many government schemes are to be selected only in the Gram Sabha. But in reality it does not happen. Beneficiaries are selected not in Gram Sabha but in Panchayat Council which is violative of the provisions of the Local Body Act of Tamil Nadu. It is a government approved unconstitutional activity. Government of Tamil Nadu emphasizes the transparent activities in all government programmes and schemes but there is no way to execute it as Gram Sabha is made defunct. It is a nightmare to many who have been enjoying power and resources all along.

Village Panchayat

A Village Panchayat or Gram Panchayat is constituted for a minimum of five hundred population. Village Panchayat can have members ranging from minimum of five to maximum of fifteen. For Village Panchayat, the ward members and the president are to be elected directly by the voters. Vice-President of the Village Panchayat is elected indirectly from among the elected ward members of the Village Panchayat. Village Panchayat has to look after the following subjects :

(a) Construction, repair and maintenance of village panchayat roads;
(b) Lighting of public roads and public places;
(c) Providing drainage facilities;
(d) Cleaning of streets;
(e) Providing public latrines;
(f) Providing burial and burning grounds;
(g) Providing water for washing and bathing purposes; and
(h) Such other duties notified by the government then and there.

To enable the village Panchayat to perform its functions the following decisions have been taken and notified through government orders:

(a) All Village Panchayats will get financial resources from the Government directly without any intermediary. Panchayati Union or Block Panchayat will not interfere in the process.
(b) Gram Panchayat Presidents have been designated as Executive Heads and they have been entrusted with powers and responsibilities.
(c) Village Panchayat roads can be taken up for construction/repair with the resolution of the Panchayat.
(d) Facilities like street light, water supply can be maintained and attended to if there is any disrepair.
(e) Part-time clerks can be appointed by the Panchayat president.
(f) House Construction plan approval has to be given by the village panchayat.
(g) Beneficiaries for the central government schemes and programmes have to be selected by the Gram Panchayat in the Gram Sabha.
(h) New library and information centre in the villages has to be established by the village panchayat.

Panchayati Union

For each development block a panchayati union is formed. Each panchayati union has a chairperson and a vice-chairperson elected indirectly by the members of the panchayat council. Union Council Members are elected directly by the people. For every 5,000 population, one union council member will be elected by the people. Members of Parliament and Legislative Assembly elected from that area are ex-officio members of the panchayat union council.

Panchayati union has the following duties and responsibilities:

(a) Construction, repair and maintenance of public roads;
(b) Establishment and maintenance of dispensaries;
(c) Construction and maintenance of elementary schools;
(d) Preventive and remedial measures connected with any epidemic;
(e) Conduct of fairs and festivals;
(f) Veterinary relief;
(g) Opening and maintenance of Panchayat Union markets;
(h) Extension of village sites and regulation of buildings;
(i) Maintenance of statistics related to births and deaths;
(j) Improvement of agriculture and agriculture stock;
(k) Promotion and encouragement of cottage industries;
(l) Other duties and responsibilities entrusted to Panchayati Union by the Government through Government notification.

To enable the panchayati union to perform its duties the Government of Tamil Nadu has issued notification to take up the following activities:

(a) Construction and maintaining Panchayat Union roads, irrigation tanks, and lakes, initiating family welfare activities, executing noon meal schemes and implementing schemes for Adi Dravidas;
(b) Works have to be identified for Employment Assurance schemes and they are to be executed;
(c) Drought relief works have to be identified and executed;
(d) M.P. and M.L.A. Area development schemes akin to union have to be executed;
(e) Panchayati union buildings have to be maintained by the union itself;
(f) Panchayat union can supervise the activities in the domain of public health, primary education,

drinking water supply, roads, small culverts, khadi and village industries works, technical training, libraries, rural electricity and non-conventional energy.

Panchayati union administrative arrangement has been modified by which works have been classified into divisions and entrusted to Block Development Officer and Assistant Block Development Officer. Two sections work independently with their supporting staff. Infrastructural facilities have also been divided and attached to two divisions.

District Panchayat

District Panchayat is constituted with the directly elected members for every 50,000 population and indirectly elected chairperson and vice-chairperson from among the council members. Members of Parliament and State Legislative Assembly of that area are the ex-officio members of the District Panchayat Council. District Panchayat will have to perform the following functions:

(a) Advise the government in all matters concerning Panchayati Raj institutions particularly on services and development programmes;
(b) Watching the progress of the measures undertaken by the government, Village panchayats and panchayati union councils in the districts as under the administrative control of the districts;
(c) Classification of markets, fairs and public roads in Panchayati Raj institutions, and
(d) Collection of data, publication of statistics, demanding any information from village panchayats and panchayati union councils.

To enable the district panchayat to perform the earmarked functions, an administrative change has been effected by which the Divisional Development Office which is nearer to the district headquarters will supervise the district panchayat activities. Yet another office which is away from the headquarters will look after auditing of the district panchayat activities and the third one will be attached to District Panchayat.

District Planning Committee

Government of Tamil Nadu shall constitute in every district a District Planning Committee to consolidate the plans prepared by the district panchayat, panchayati union councils, village panchayats, municipal councils, and municipal corporations in the district and to prepare a draft development plan for the district as a whole. The committee shall consist of the Collector of the district, members of the House of the People who represent whole or part of the district, members of the council of State, members of legislative assembly whose constituencies lie within the district, Mayor of the city municipal corporation and all chairpersons of the municipalities of the district, chairperson of the district panchayat, one fifth of the total number of chairpersons of town panchayats and panchayati union notified by the government every year by rotation, and such number of persons not less than four-fifth of the total number of the committees as specified by the government elected from among the members of district panchayat, town panchayats, municipal councils and corporations in the district in proportion to the ratio between the population of the rural areas and of the urban areas. The District Collector is the Chairperson, district panchayat president is the vice-chairperson and chief executive officer of the district panchayat is the secretary of the district planning committee. The committee shall allocate funds for various schemes to the panchayats and panchayat union and shall monitor the implementation of schemes.

Reservation

One-third of positions at all levels of the bodies are reserved for women. SC and ST get reservation of positions at all levels of the bodies in proportion to their population.

Election and Finance Commissions

An Election Commission headed by the State Election Commissioner appointed by the Governor to conduct the local body elections is mandatory. The election commissioner enjoys powers, privileges and status of a judge of the High Court. The tenure of office of the election commissioner is two years. However, the commissioner can be given extension for four more years.

There will be a Finance Commission constituted every fifth year to review financial position of the panchayats and to make recommendations to the Governor as to fix the principles to govern the distribution between the State and panchayats of the net proceeds of the taxes, duties, tolls and fees leviable by the Government which may be divided between them and allocation between the district panchayats, panchayat union councils and village panchayats of their respective shares of such proceeds. Further to identify the logistics for making grants-in-aid to the panchayats from the consolidated fund of the State and the measures needed to improve the financial position of the panchayats. The Finance Commission shall consist of a chairman and four other members.

Critical Evaluation[9]

But these provisions have been made ineffective and sometimes inoperative with immunity. The major defects in the Act are:

1. Subjects in the 11th Schedule do not find a place in the body of the Act especially in the chapter on functions of panchayati bodies;
2. Development officials, who work in the Panchayati bodies, are declared as government officials and they do not come under the purview of local bodies;
3. District Collector is vested with power of controlling the Village Panchayats. District Collector has the power to suspend and dissolve the Gram Panchayat arbitrarily;

4. DRDA a registered society operating huge amount of Rural Development activities resources under the control of the district collector and it is not under the purview of Panchayati bodies;
5. Fixing one-third of members of Gram Sabha as quorum has made the Panchayati leaders unable to convene the Gram Sabha as it is very difficult to ensure the quorum;
6. No proper linkages between Gram Panchayat and Panchayati Union, Panchayati Union and District Panchayat;
7. Very limited powers are given to Panchayats to mobilize resources on their own.

Though the Act was passed, efforts were not on to conduct the election to local bodies till the DMK party came to power.

The eleventh general election has drawn the attention of the political parties towards the new Panchayati Raj System. Dravida Munnetra Kazhagam had prominently highlighted the failure of the AIADMK in conducting the election to local bodies and it promised the people in its manifesto that it would conduct the election to local bodies immediately if it returns to power.[10] After it came to power, at a stroke it conducted the election to the local bodies both urban and rural after issuing an ordinance authorizing withdrawal of the provision to reserve seats for backward class in the local bodies. Certain changes have been introduced in the system of Tamil Nadu local bodies by the DMK Government before the conduct of the election. Gram Panchayat has been freed from the clutches of the political parties, and the provision of drawing one-fifth of representatives from Gram Panchayats to Block Panchayats, from Block Panchayats to District Panchayat has been withdrawn.

After the election, the elected representatives to local bodies from varied strata of the society with high hopes and aspirations went into the portals of power.

During electioneering the media have highlighted the importance, implication of local bodies and the increasing monetary flow to local bodies which probably drew the attention of all sections to participate in the electoral process. As electioneering process demanded money, candidates who have contested the election had to spend money. Thus the candidates have spent the money with the hope that they can take it back from the schemes that are going to be implemented through their respective bodies and the beneficiaries. Post-election scenario has projected a dismal picture about the activities of the leaders as the officials went on carrying out their works unmindful of the leaders who have been elected. The officials without having any guidance from the State Government acted in a manner which is to their advantage by using the provisions available in the old Act and tried their level best to involve the elected leaders in the contract system to perform certain development works sponsored by both the State and the Central Governments.

In the meanwhile the cry for power has been vociferous and as a result a meeting of local body leaders was convened by the Chief Minister immediately after the election and the elected leaders were asked to express their difficulties. In fact the leaders explained their position that they have no power and resource and they are not respected by the officials and their words have not been given due weightage in the offices and of course they demanded certain facilities for themselves as the local body leaders enjoy elsewhere. Finally the Chief Minister delivered his speech with a pessimistic note. Yet the cry for power has not come to an end and instead it has increased. The local body leaders formed associations and discussed their problems and sent their resolutions to the Government.

Moreover, Union Finance Minister P. Chidambaram and the opposition leader in the State Legislative Assembly S. Balakrishnan have joined issue with the Chief Minister on the procrastination of the State government in devolving powers and resources to the local bodies. People's expectations from the leaders of local bodies have increased and hence the representatives of the local bodies have been pressurised by the people for services and facilities to the people. Having understood the restlessness of the local body leaders the Government of Tamil Nadu have appointed a committee under the chairmanship of L.C. Jain to workout the modalities of transferring power and resources to local bodies. The committee has submitted an interim report to enable the government to devolve powers so as to make the panchayats take up works for providing facilities and services to the people.[11] Before passing the recommendations and issuing G.O. the leaders have been made to fight against each other by making use of the loopholes in the arrangement of the structure.

In Tamil Nadu Panchayati Raj system, the Gram Panchayat comprises directly elected president and ward members and indirectly elected vice-president. The Block Panchayat comprises directly elected ward members and indirectly elected chairperson and vice-chairperson. Zilla parishad consists of directly elected ward members and indirectly elected president and vice-president. The very purpose of creating this structure is to make each unit an autonomous body to tackle certain problems depending on their capacity. But in reality each tier is working against another due to duplication of work and duality of the roles. The Gram Panchayat has its own jurisdiction of work. But the Block panchayat ward members hailing from the same place claim that they are equivalent to Gram Panchayat president and hence they demand certain specific powers on par with the president. On the same basis Zilla Parishad members also claim the same. They demand powers equivalent to those of the president of Block Panchayat.

In reality nobody knows which body has what powers? Acts, decisions, policies are put into practice only through Government orders. Government officials have not received any order from the government of Tamil Nadu till October 1996. Restlessness of the leaders of local bodies has increased and it compelled the State authorities to take initiative to devolve powers. The State Government exerted pressure on the Planning Commission and especially on L.C. Jain to submit his interim report and thereby an interim report was submitted. In the meanwhile the elected leaders have been asked to undergo one day training conducted by the officials. Dos and don'ts have been read in the programme and it had not invoked any interest among the leaders. Finally in the month of October 1996, an order was issued by the Government of Tamil Nadu. The G.O. issued by the Government has taken nearabout four months to reach the Gram Panchayat presidents. Even in the G.O. the Government has not stated any original function for the panchayats. It has mentioned only agency functions.

Implementing schemes of the federal government is mentioned as powers of the panchayats. After issuing the government order the presidents of Gram Panchayats have been made to act as contractors. Beneficiaries of schemes have to be selected by the Gram Sabha. When this is the practice, as per the provision of the Act the ward members of Panchayati Union demanded such role for them. When the schemes were allotted to Block, Zilla Panchayat members demanded such powers to carry out certain works under the schemes sponsored by the Central Government. Thus the elected representatives of local bodies have developed a perception that they have to carry out the programmes and schemes of the federal and State government without knowing the original functions of the local body institutions.

It is interesting to note that the representatives of the people in the local bodies have imbibed the qualities of the MLAs and MPs and have been acting in the same way as MLAs and MPs are behaving and performing in their respective constituencies. MPs are working in the local bodies through their local area development scheme with an amount of one crore rupees and MLAs are working in the local bodies through their scheme with an amount of twenty-five lakh rupees for an year, This has reduced the importance of the representatives of the local bodies. Since local body institutions have enormous amount of money to be spent, interference of the representatives will be frequent and intense.

The local body leaders do not know the background of the 73rd Amendment to the Constitution of India, main provisions of the amendment, key provisions of the State Act, major schemes of the both the federal and provincial government, availability of resources, and process of micro level planning as has been inferred from a variety of need-assessment studies.[12] As candidates contesting for Assembly and Parliament election, the candidates have contested for the local body election. After the election, the elected representatives without knowing the full implications of the local bodies started functioning as liaison between the people and the officials. They consider local body institutions as political institutions instead of development institutions.

The Government also slowly have enabled the elected representatives to enjoy the comforts as MLAs and MPs enjoy. Before giving any clearcut power and responsibility, the State government have provided one Ambassador car to the president of Zilla Panchayat. He has been provided with a good office in the collectorate without any power to take decision in the functioning of the development institutions in the collectorate such as a district rural development agency. Likewise Tata Sumo a luxury van has been provided to every Block Panchayat which is being used by the Panchayati Union chairperson. Perks have been announced for the local body leaders. Sitting fees and travel concessions have been fixed with ceiling for the local body institutions.

While the representatives of the people have been in full swing in sharing the responsibility of executing the schemes and programmes of the State and central governments, Government of Tamil Nadu has issued an ordinance making district collector as chairperson of District Planning Committee. To protest against this decision, L.C. Jain, member of the State Planning Commission tendered his resignation. This has sensitised the leaders of various political parties and they have demanded that District Panchayat president should be made the chairperson of the District Planning Committee. Still this controversy has not been resolved. As a result of intensive criticism the Government of Tamil Nadu has come out with a decision to constitute another committee of representatives of all political parties to go into the details of the problems akin to devolution of power. In the meanwhile L.C. Jain has submitted his report.[13] Government orders have been issued.[14]

Inferences

DMK is the ruling party in the province of Tamil Nadu. In the local bodies DMK has gained major portion of seats along with TMC. Yet there is reluctance on the part of the leaders to devolve powers to local bodies. This unwillingness to part with power to local body leaders by the State Government has created a lurking fear among the local body leaders that the Panchayati Raj institutions will be disturbed covertly and overtly. The local body leaders are oriented towards politics rather than towards development. They have started doing agency functions without knowing their original functions. Contractors are replaced by the elected leaders, without proper capacity building exercise and hence the local body leaders find it difficult to perform their role. There is no scope for micro level planning in the present arrangement of devolution of powers.

The local bodies have no control over the resources. Their share in the resource mobilization is very limited. Dissemination of information is very rare among the leaders. MPs and MLAs schemes have limited the scope of local body leaders activities in the rural areas. There is inadequate intellectual input to the local body institutions. The officials who are performing the role connected with the subjects earmarked for Panchayati Raj institutions are reluctant to come under the jurisdiction of the local bodies due to the lukewarm attitude of the State level leaders and the government. Thus, the Panchayati Raj in Tamil Nadu is not an institution of self-governance.

Conclusion

Local body institutions are at the mercy of the State Government for their functioning with powers and adequate resources. The very logic of decentralization of power is lost sight of. From the available perception it is inferred that local bodies are viewed as agents to carry out the schemes and programmes of the federal and State governments. The State level leaders perceive that the sudden devolution of powers would decentralise corruption. This situation necessitated an array of actions, namely :

1. Awareness creation among the people about the New Panchayati Raj System;
2. Enhancing the capacity of the newly elected leaders to discharge their functions; and
3. Resource identification and resource transfer to local bodies.

These issues have to be tackled expeditiously and political support base has to be created to devolve powers to local bodies in the absence of political will on the part of the leaders at the State level. The existing laws which act as deterrents to the main provision of the Panchayati Raj Act are to be modified. The institutional mechanism to empower the leaders to manage the institutions must be developed which will be the only option available at present.

Notes and References

1. Steps have been taken to take stock of the situation at different levels. Institute of Social Sciences, New Delhi, Rajiv Gandhi Foundation, New Delhi, Ford Foundation, New Delhi, Voluntary Organisations Network, Indian Institute of Public Administration and the Ministry of Rural Areas and Employment have involved themselves in the process of revitalising grassroots democracy. Specifically in Rajiv Gandhi Foundation, a task force on Panchayati Raj has been constituted to monitor the progress of the New Panchayati Raj System. Rajiv Gandhi Foundation, *Revitalisation of Panchayati Raj in India*, New Delhi : RGF, 1997.
2. Michael M.Cernea (ed.), *Putting People First:Sociological Variables in Rural Development Projects*, New York; Oxford University Press, 1985.
3. George Mathew, *New Panchayati Raj System: From Legislation to Movement*, New Delhi : Concept Publications, 1996.
4. For a detailed analysis see department of Rural Development, *Powers and Functions of Panchayati Raj Institutions: A Framework*, New Delhi : Ministry of Rural Areas and Employment, 1994.
5. Ministry of Rural Areas and Employment, *73rd Constitutional Amendment Act*, New Delhi : Ministry of Rural Areas and

Employment, 1993.

6. LRSA, *The Politics of Panchayati Raj*, Chengalpattu: Legal Resources for Social Action, 1990.
7. Government of Tamil Nadu, *Tamil Nadu Local Bodies Act, 1994.* Chennai : Publication Division, 1995.
8. S.S. Singh, Suresh Mishra and Sanjay Pratap, *Legislative Status of Panchayati Raj in India*, New Delhi : Indian Institute of Public Administration, 1997, pp. 457-79.
9. The steps that can be taken to bring the Tamil Nadu Act in line with 73rd Constitutional Amendment Act have been suggested through a document. For more details see Department of Political Science, *From Participation to Self-Governance*, Gandhigram: Department of Political Science and Development Administration, 1998.
10. DMK, *Manifesto of the Dravida Munnetra Kazhagam*, Madras: Party Publication, 1996.
11. State Planning Commission, *Interim Report on the Entrustment of Powers to Panchayats*, Chennai: State Planning Commission, 1997.
12. G. Palanithurai, *Have our hopes belied?* Gandhigram:Rajiv Gandhi Chair for Panchayati Raj Studies, 1997.
13. State Planning Commission, *Report on the Entrustment of Powers to Panchayats*, Chennai : State Planning Commission, 1997.
14. Department of Rural Development, *Responsibilities and Powers handed over to Panchayats*, Chennai : Government of Tamil Nadu, 1998.

9

Conflicting Roles in Representative Institutions

Functional Overlapping

The executive decision to earmark an amount of money to members of Parliament under the caption "MPs Local Area Development Programme" and subsequently the decision of the State government to earmark Rs. 35 lakhs to MLAs for the same purpose have questioned the very logic of the separation of powers between legislatures and executives. Subtly at a higher level of analysis and understanding, the marked departure of the legislative institutions to move into the domain of executive functions is felt. But in reality and in the field it is a competition and conflict among the representatives of the people to perform certain functions and to allocate resources from the earmarked fund for carrying out suitable schemes and programmes.

In the governing process of the three-tier structure of the representative institutions, one would find more responsiveness in terms of redressing the grievances of the people as large number of representatives are in the field with power and resources. The problem arises only when the representatives of all the three tiers of the political system, namely, parliament, legislature and local bodies perform certain overlapping functions and develop conflict among themselves in competing with each other to perform the same job.[1]

Basic Questions

Parliament, provincial legislatures and local bodies have to perform their role and function in the respective spheres. The representative institutions have to discharge their duties as earmarked in the Constitution.[2] When such is the case how would their functions overlap? MPs, MLAs, members of local bodies are trying to perform the same role in the constituencies. Moreover, they compete with each other in attending some of the problems and issues of the people as the earmarked money is with district collectors and sometimes it has been noticed that adequate resources are available. However, the representatives do not find issues and problems to spend the money on. An example could be quoted here to demonstrate the reality from a district of Tamil Nadu. Representatives, namely, MP, MLA and local bodies of Dindigul district recommended that road works have to be taken up for execution. All the representatives recommended the same road. Almost all the roads which are to be undertaken for repair have been repaired but even then they have excess money. In Tamil Nadu, similar to the money earmarked for MPs and MLAs, money has also been earmarked for members of District Panchayat, and Block Panchayats instead of responsibilities. In the same way members of Gram Panchayat demand allocation of money for them too. The works are distributed to all in order to spend the money for various activities. Mostly local body works have been distributed among the representatives of the people in different bodies. It is obvious from the reports that there is no question of dearth of money. Equally the issues and problems too are abundant. But there is no match between the money and the problems.

Theoretical Underpinnings

The existing conditions indicate a few theoretical underpinnings. In a representative form of government, the representatives have certain earmarked representational roles such as interest aggregation and interest articulation.[3] The representatives have to aggregate the demands and grievances of the people and articulate the same in the appropriate authoritative bodies for policy making, decision making and money allocation. Hence their understanding of the issues and problems and their presentation of those issues in such bodies would bring necessary decision and resources if they are done properly. When decisions, policies and money allocations are made properly in these bodies the problems of the people would be solved easily. In India decisions are taken, policies and money allocations are made but yet the problems remain unsolved. Consequently the institutions get increasing volume of demands from the people. Demands of the people vary in dimension, nature and volume. Demands akin to issues, regions, constituencies and individuals are getting aggregated and articulated in authoritative bodies.[4] In India it has been reported that heavy volume of individual demands have been projected. When greater amount of demands are projected and such a trend continues, it will be an indication of the poor response of the government to the issues of the people. Parliament and Legislatures are witnessing projection of more localised, individualistic demands which could be solved at lower levels through the institutions available below the State Legislature.[5]

The ongoing transformation in the Legislature-Executive relationship indicates the failure of the legislative institutions in performing their representational role and function in evolving suitable policy options to meet the growing demands of the people.[6] Likewise, the executive has also failed in its function in implementing the legislative decisions successfully. While evolving a suitable institutional mechanism to remedy the existing situation, they found out the local body institution. In the new context, the local body institutions are to be equipped with new responsibilities. The new assignments to local body leaders with increased resources to them have caused panic among the MLAs and MPs that the tie-up arrangement between the local body leaders and the people is much more stronger than the relationship between MLAs, MPs and the people. Hence they have demanded such allocations to the MPs and MLAs.

The Case of Tamil Nadu

To meet the unmet requirements of the people, people's representatives in the local bodies demanded allocation of money exclusively for them. MPs and MLAs are projecting the same demand.[7] MLAs of some of the States have been granted the financial allocation exclusively for them and rules and regulations have been evolved to spend the money for constituency development activities. The activities indicated in the list earmarked for MPs and MLAs are not different from the activities of the local bodies. Now in Tamil Nadu MPs and MLAs are operating the fund along with local body institutions. Even after operating all those funds, the needs and problems of the people are still unmet.

In a village, funds are being operated by various agencies on different development programmes. Village Panchayat presidents are operating schemes, Block panchayat is also implementing schemes earmarked for Block panchayats and District panchayats are also operating certain programmes in the villages. Even the programmes of the three-tier panchayats are not properly integrated. Apart from these programmes and schemes of the local bodies, MPs and MLAs are also operating their schemes. So in a village five types of schemes are being implemented. Neither the panchayati president nor the people are aware of which scheme is being operated by whom and for what purpose. The basic question here is, has the multiplicity of programmes solved the problems of the people?[8]

There is competition between MLAs and MPs and among the representatives of people in the local bodies in operating programmes and schemes. One would find conflicts also among the representatives in operating schemes. The present conditions generate demands from the representatives that they should be given some funds to operate. Moreover, the perks and privileges of the MPs and MLAs propelled the local body leaders to put forth a demand of such privileges and perks to them, proportionate to the works done by them in their respective constituencies.

The works carried out in the rural areas under various

schemes are not known to the people as people are not consulted whether the work is needed for the community or not. These works are being implemented by the contractors. There is no coordination among the representatives of the people in executing the schemes and programmes operated in a district. In each district, on an average, 1.3 MPs, 8.06 MLAs are operating their funds to the tune of Rs. 4.12 crores for development activities.

243(G) is the operating clause of the 73rd Constitutional Amendment which says that economic development and social justice are the prime objectives of the new dispensation of grassroots level governance. The underpinnings of the objectives reiterate the importance of planning at the grassroots level with the participation of the people for economic development and social justice. When planning at the local level for total development, local body institutions are an imperative for operation of independent programmes and schemes which are highly irrelevant and not helpful to achieve economic growth and social equity.[9]

For economic development and social justice, mere increasing of infrastructural facilities will not help. Apart from infrastructural facilities, creating employment opportunities at the local level is the vital need. At the local level, planning has to be initiated to meet the basic needs and to facilitate the local community in order to create employment opportunities by making use of the resources received from the governments and other funding agencies along with the resources mobilised by the local bodies on their own. Hence all the resources have to be pooled and shared for integrated actvities. But in reality resources in Tamil Nadu are utilized to provide infrastructural facilities not in an integrated fashion. Moreover, attending the works under various schemes is not based on the needs but because the money is available at various levels. In the new dispensation of decentralised governance, eliminating contract system forms part of administering development. Since allocations are made for representatives and options are given to them to indicate their preference in selecting works within the menu of works, it is easy for them to choose works which are to be implemented through contractors and thereby the representatives could find money for their political activities. The present arrangement for allocation of works and resources for development activities provides opportunities for corruption.[10]

Yet another problem is the proliferation of rules and regulations governing the operation of schemes and programmes for local bodies. MPs and MLAs are having one crore and thirty-five lakhs of rupees for constituency development activities respectively. In order to spend the money, the members of Parliament and Legislatures can indicate the works to the Collector. No responsibility is vested with the legislators with regard to the implementation of schemes and programmes, whereas the local body leaders are responsible for implementing programmes and schemes. Each and every work account has to be maintained by the local body leaders. Higher amount of resources have been earmarked for higher level representatives with less accountability. On the contrary the local/grassroots level leaders have greater responsibilities and demands but they are given very less amount with several stipulations and conditions. Gram Panchayati presidents have been watching the schemes and programmes carried out by different representatives through their contractors but the presidents of Gram Panchayats are implementing programmes and schemes in the villages on their own and they are accountable to the works done by them. Moreover, they have to strictly follow the guidelines given by the government. A Gram Panchayati president has to follow thirty-three types of separate accounts and procedures while implementing schemes.[11]

Higher level representatives seem to be involved in local body activities and not accountable to the people. They have perks and privileges on the higher side, more allocation of schemes but local body leaders have more works, tight rules and regulations less amount of perks and privileges. People are demanding more facilities from the local body leaders as they are easily approachable and closer to the people. Since the contractors are operating certain works in the villages from the allocation given by the MLAs and MPs, the working arrangement is between the representatives and the contractors. Nobody questions the contractors but the works carried out by the Gram Panchayat leaders are supervised and questioned by the people. As long as the contractors are operating programmes and schemes, bribes will be given by the contractors to the bureaucrats and representatives. Local body leaders especially Gram Panchayati presidents carry out works directly and they issue cheque directly to the persons responsible for work. Bureaucracy demands money for each and every scheme. There is a fixed percentage for the bureaucracy. Like the MPs and MLAs local body leaders have also spent money for election and how they would manage the money from the schemes is a problem, since people are alert and closer to the local bodies in Tamil Nadu.

Conclusion

Rules and regulations for the conduct of the business of the Houses are clear for both the Parliament and Legislatures. Likewise powers are also clear for both governments at the Centre and the States. However, for local bodies no such clear-cut rules and regulations and powers exist for the three-tier institutions. After the enactment of the 73rd Constitutional Amendment and granting of money to MPs and MLAs for local area development, redefining the role of the Members of Parliament and State Legislatures as well the leaders of local bodies is an imperative. Moreover, rethinking on resource allocation made to MPs and MLAs under "Local area development programme" is needed. Allocation of money to representatives is not a sound practice in a system. To set right the malaise in the dynamics of the system, earmarking a clear-cut role at various layers of the authoritative bodies from Gram Panchayat to parliament to the representatives and training them in discharging their duties and responsibilities is indispensable proposal in the present context.

Notes and References

1. G. Palanithurai, *Report of the Training Programme for Gram Panchayati Presidents of Dindigul and Sivaganga Districts*, Gandhigram : Rajiv Gandhi Chair, 1998.
2. Michael L. Mezey, "The Functions of Legislatures in the Third World" in *Handbook of Legislative Research* (eds.) Gerald Loewenberg, Samuel C. Patterson and Malcolm E. Jewell, Cambridge: Harvard University Press, 1985.
3. Michael L. Mezey, *Comparative Legislatures*, Durham:Duke University Press, 1979, pp. 145-220.
4. For more details, see Peter H. Merkl, *Modern Comparative Politics*, Illinois:The Dryden Press, 1977, pp. 92-128.
5. S.R. Maheswari, "Constituency Linkage of National Legislators in India", *Legislative Studies Quarterly*, 1 (Aug, 1976), 331-54.
6. G. Palanithurai, *The Role Perception of Legislators: A Case Study of Tamil Nadu*, New Delhi:Konark Publications, 1991.
7. Candidates contesting the general election project more of local issues which are coming under the purview of local bodies.
8. This question has been elaborately discussed in the Interface programme organised by Rajiv Gandhi Foundation in Kerala Institute of Local Administration in Trissur. For more details, see Rajiv Gandhi Foundation, *Group Report of Colloquia on Decentralised Governance, Political Economy and Administration* (Southern States), New Delhi: RGF, 1998.
9. Department of Political Science, *From Participation to Self-Governance*, Gandhigram: Department of Political Science, 1998.
10. G. Palanithurai, *Containing Corruption at the Micro-level: An Experiment*, Gandhigram: Rajiv Gandhi Chair, 1998 (Mimeo).
11. For more details, see G. Palanithurai, *New Panchayati Raj System at Work: An Evaluation*, New Delhi: Concept Publications, 1998.

10
Self-Governance sans Controls

What is going on in the rural areas under the active headship of the local body leaders is nothing but implementing the schemes and programmes of the Government of India and Tamil Nadu. Leaders have been oriented by the officials to implement the schemes and programmes and thereby the mind-set of the leaders has been on getting money for the assigned and earmarked works irrespective of whether the villagers need those schemes or not. Huge amount of money has been spent on various schemes and yet the felt needs of the people have not been met. To meet the needs of the people the leaders of the panchayats demand powers and resources from the State government. As they don't get their legitimate powers, they continue to demand powers and perform their tasks as agents without going much deeper into the original functions of local bodies as per the Acts. The officials on their part have proliferated rules and procedures for implementing schemes and programmes of the government and handed over the same to the local body leaders especially the Gram Panchayat presidents. This has ultimately developed a fear in their minds and thereby they have to be under the control of the officials and sometimes even at the beck and call of the panchayat clerk. Though the quantum of money has been increased the operational dimension of the panchayats is severely crippled due to the cumbersome procedures and rules in the backdrop of the educational and social background of the leaders. The revolution in rising expectations among the people propelled the leaders of local bodies to put forth demands for more resources from the State and Central governments and more powers to deal with the situation locally. Further the allocation of funds for MPs and MLAs for local area development schemes made the local body leaders to put forth such demands in terms of money. From MP to Gram Panchayat president, all the representatives continue to make such demands, namely, access to resources and powers. Nobody talked about responsibilities. By demanding powers and resources, representatives start quarrelling against each other. Institutional arrangements of the three tiers for governance are so designed as to create conflict among themselves and thus local body institutions are created not as self-governing institutions but as agents of Central and State governments to implement their programmes.

Local body institutions have two sets of functions, namely, the original and the agency. Original functions are: taking decisions, mobilizing resources, implementing their decisions and programmes based on their planning and evaluating the same. Agency functions are: implementing the programmes and schemes of the Central and State governments. So far panchayati institutions have been performing agency functions alone. But after the enactment of the 73rd and 74th Amendments to the Constitutions of India, the nature of the functions of local bodies has been changed.

But the mind-set of the leaders, people and bureaucracy is the same on local bodies as of the agents to implement the programmes and schemes of Central and State governments and more particularly it has to provide only services to the people as it had done the same for long in India. Unless the mind-set is changed it is very difficult to bring the needed change in the functioning of the grassroots level institutions.

To bring a change in the mind-set of the leaders of local bodies, Gandhigram Rural Institute has taken up the assignment of conducting training for Gram Panchayati presidents with the financial support of the Ministry of Rural Areas and Employment, Government of India. It is mainly intended to enhance the capacity of the people's representatives.

The ongoing training programme for Gram Panchayat presidents brings a lot of information for our understanding of the local body institutions. Two hundred and fifty-five presidents have participated in the training programme and of whom none said that they know the full details of 73rd amendment to the Constitution of India. None expressed that they are aware of the main provisions of the Tamil Nadu Panchayat Act of 1994. What is surprising is that they know a few programmes of the Central government as they are currently being operated through DRDA. Apart from this they know nothing about socio-economic implications of the new institutional arrangement of governance at the local level.

They contested in the election as candidates used to contest for MLA or MP in the general election without knowing the full implications of representative institutions in a democratic government. For MLAs and MPs well-laid procedures are there to perform their role and function. But the newly created local bodies have to depend on the new legislation enacted in the year 1994 which is considered as one of the most backward Acts in India. Committees have been set up to make recommendations to fix the powers to be devolved from the State government to local bodies among the three tiers of the same. Government orders have been issued slowly to earmark responsibilities to local bodies and yet, local bodies are not clear as to the functions they are to perform. The government of Tamil Nadu has been implementing schemes and programmes of the federal government intensively for more than two decades and the same have been distributed among the three tiers of the panchayati institutions. It has come to a stage to believe that the local body institutions have to implement the programmes and schemes of both the State and Central governments. Hence the local body leaders feel that more amount of money has to come from the government, and adequate powers have to be given to the local bodies to execute the same.

In the past two years the Gram Panchayati presidents specifically and others in other two tiers of panchayati institutions generally have been oriented by the officials in the course of their regular interaction that the panchayati bodies have been created to implement schemes and programme of the State and Central governments. 243(G) of the 73rd constitutional amendment Act does not find any significance in their dealings and this provision was not brought to light in the functions of panchayat in the past two years. But contrarily people in the rural areas have developed expectation that the local bodies have to provide more facilities through programmes and schemes than MLA and MP and moreover, these expectations are due to the promises given by the representatives without knowing much details about the provisions of the new Panchayati Raj Act. Local body leaders have given promises to the people as the MLAs and MPs. MLAs and MPs can escape from the people as they meet their constituents rarely and they live far away from them but the local body leaders are with the people and hence every day people would raise demands. Thus the elected leaders of the local bodies face a lot of problems as they have given tall promises which cannot be fulfilled in the given framework of the functioning of Local bodies.

MLAs and MPs re-election is purely based on the performance of their political parties and their leaders. Therefore, even without attending the routine works, they can win the election, if their party and its leaders have a good image among the people. But re-election of local body leaders is purely based on their performance as they are working closely with people. Performance of the local body leaders are properly evaluated by the people.

It is proper that the local bodies have to assess the needs of the people and identify the priorities. After the proper assessment of the needs, planning has to be initiated. To meet the expenditure, panchayats have to find out resources not only from the State and Central governments but also from other sources. Ways and means have to be found out to enable the people to participate in each and every programme of the panchayats from planning to implementation and evaluation of programmes and schemes. In each and every programme or scheme contribution of the beneficiaries either in resource or in labour must be made compulsory to ensure the success of the programme. To carry out the planned schemes and programmes, they need responsible individuals and groups from the panchayats. To plan, mobilise resources and to execute the schemes panchayat needs powers. Powers are to discharge the responsibilities. But the present day local body leaders are mad after power and resources. They talk much about powers rather than responsibilities.

The day-to-day transactions are in contradiction to the basic principles of the new panchayati system. The federal government has given schemes and money which have been handed over to local bodies. Since they have schemes and programmes, they are to be implemented irrespective of their need. Whether the village needs the retaining wall or not they are taken up for implementation since it is sanctioned. As a result, felt needs are unmet and schemes are continued to be executed. Village panchayat presidents are projecting a series of demands and seeking money from the government to meet those basic demands. But the officials continue to say no to their demands as there is no such provision in financial outlay. Most of the presidents do believe that they can get more benefits from the government and give them to the people. They do not feel that they are change agents and they have more onerous responsibilities.

Even in implementing schemes and programmes officials stipulate conditions and procedures which are to be adhered to strictly to maintain financial discipline. Since panchayat presidents have not been trained to perform their duties and discharge their responsibilities within the framework of rules, most of the time they accuse the officials for laying down conditions and stipulation. It is also true that the rules and regulations governing the schemes and programmes are too much for the poor dalit presidents and especially women presidents to understand and act accordingly. They are allergic towards such rules and regulations and the local body leaders mostly rely on the help of the panchayati clerk and the officials working in panchayati union. Women presidents mostly depend on their husbands to discharge their responsibilities.

Genuinely they feel that they are being helped by their husbands.

Yet another problem they face in the village is the competition among the groups to share the benefits of the schemes and programmes of the government. People look at the benefits of the government from their own perspective without considering the stipulations of the government to grant benefits to the people. People also believe that panchayati institutions are political institutions and hence the leaders should exert their influence to get things done for the people belonging to the party affiliation of the president irrespective of the rules and regulations. People feel that each and every issue has to be decided politically in the present context. As a result there is a likelihood of cornering all the benefits of the government by the dominant elements of the villages.

Gram Sabha is the Parliament of the Gram Panchayat where people get to know what is going on in the village in terms of development and what is to be done in the village in the future and people have to ventilate their feelings and demands. It is not only a place for mere exchange of ideas and articulating the grievances of the people but to evolve solutions to the problems they face in the village on their own. The very basic idea of Gram Sabha is to create a feeling of community and to ensure people's participation in the development process.

The refusal of the Gram Panchayat presidents to convene Gram Sabha meeting is due to the fact that the people look at the panchayat as the political institution not as development institution. Hence people would raise questions on any matter and issues based on party consideration. Moreover it is very difficult to manage several hundred people in a particular place especially in a village settlement where there is no organisational stipulation and regulation to manage the crowd.

Yet another major problem they face is the prevalence of corruption in the implementation process of the schemes and programmes for rural development. Everyone talks about corruption, nobody suggests ways and means to control it. People in the rural areas are affected in many ways directly due to the corrupt practices adopted by the officials. Even to get a community certificate one has to bribe the revenue officials. People are not able to get their entitlements from the fair price shop. To get the schemes and programmes panchayati presidents have to give money to officials. Just like a service charge the officials fix rates for each and every scheme and programme. If the president refuses to pay, bills for works done will not be passed for payment by the officials. Panchayati presidents feel that the Union Engineer is the most corrupt person in the whole arrangement of the development process. So there is no way out for the panchayati presidents to escape from this menace. Another version of the same story is that the presidents who have spent a lot for the election are planning to take back money from the schemes and programmes and hence the officials seek their share from them only and not from all. If the Gram Panchayat presidents are honest and sincere, they need not bother about the officials and they can perform their functions without any hindrance.

The whole disease is the outcome of distorted perception of the people and their leaders that the panchayats are government-sponsored institutions and not the institutions of the people. If the panchayats are made as institutions of the people, most of the ills could be eliminated easily. What is needed at this juncture is the right perception about the new system and the will to perform their duties and responsibilities on the part of the grassroot level leaders to make the local body institutions as institutions of self-governance sans controls from the Central and State governments.

11

Containing Corruption

A Micro Experiment

A. DISCUSSION

This chapter seeks some clarification from the available knowledge and literature on corruption. Corruption, as a major phenomenon in the political sphere, has been discussed for a long time. Even before 1990, corruption had been in the agenda of the political parties especially during the time of election. This type of outburst among the political parties has sometimes provoked the administration to act on the memoranda submitted by the leaders of various political parties. As a result, in the middle of 1980's a twelve-volume series entitled "Committees and Commissions on Corruption" has been published. Yet there was no serious debate among the academics on this issue and there was no initiation of any professional body to tackle this problem. But now a new intellectual trend has been set in motion in Indian academia. Why this fervour now? And a fervour among the intellectuals?

A Lead from Lending Agency

As long as the money generated from within has been put in the pipeline for various activities of the government and there were leakages in the pipeline (leakage or seepage has to be decided on the quantum of money that has been taken away from the pipeline), none paid serious attention to it. This intellectual trend has been the outcome of a serious deliberation on the part of a funding agency which has pumped a huge amount of money for development activities in our country. When the flow of money was not properly channelised and it was mismanaged, the funding agencies expressed their anguish and dissatisfaction. Against this background, this phenomenon has been incorporated in the report of their organisations.

Funding agencies with their grants to various institutions sensitized the scholars who have been under the influence of classical liberal school especially from the West. Why this fervour only from this school? It is an open argument that funds have been allocated liberally by the funding agencies from the West, especially the USA, to the academic institutions. There is yet another question, does it mean the other school of social science, namely the Marxist is silent on it and has not taken any effort? It is not so. Why then the academics of this school through the funding of the Indian State have not taken serious note of the problems? The answers are two-fold: i.e., (1) State has not provided so much of money for this kind of exercises due to their reluctance as it would destabilize the State itself; (2) majority of Indian academics have switched over to the victorious school of classical liberalism after the end of an ideology, namely, after the collapse of communism in Russia. Yet piecemeal studies have been conducted individually and published in the journals which did not evoke the expected reaction from the academia. It could be noticed even in the trend report of the ICSSR. The ICSSR sponsored `trend report' has not projected this problem as a major issue or item for investigation.

Masking Conceptualization

Normally the academics who belong to the classical liberal school of the West used to go about any issue based on clear-cut conceptualization. But whereas in the case of corruption, after the publication of the World Bank report, corruption became a significant issue for discussion. To them leakage of money in the implementation process of the programmes is corruption. When enormous amount of money is being spent on various programmes of development, the funding agencies expect results as an endproduct of their investment. In this connection, they have indicated the corruption in terms of money taken out of the process. Since funding has been provided by the same agencies to discuss the dimensions of this issue of corruption with the set of objectives, our academics have taken up this issue without proper grounding in the form of suitable theory as they lack proper conceptualization.

While initiating our discussion from the very concept itself one has to face several problems. There are at least, two problems one has to face. Normally any violation of established law to perform a function in a given role of an individual is to be considered for the definition of the concept corruption. Likewise any violation of social norm accepted by the community can also be considered for definition. Laws, rules and regulations have been changed based on the pressure of the community. Social norms continue to face challenges in the society in the context of social change and modernisation. When social values and common laws are getting changed, the possibility for anchorage of any such definition is remote. At present there are established propositions like that corruption increases the speed of the organizations and institutions in terms of their output. Yet another question is how laws and values are regarded by the people? This aspect has to be studied deeply.

How do we take the citizen whether they are abiding by the rules and regulations of the society and government or not? It is ultimately realised on the nature of the State and perception of the people about a problem. When Gandhiji expressed his opinion about corruption at the dawn of Independence nobody worried much about it. When commissions had been constituted to probe into the allegations against the government, people believed that based on the findings of the commissions and committees, action would be initiated against the guilty. But things were different after the submission of reports of commissions. It becomes an issue for politics. The authority which constituted the committees and commissions has got the power to take or not to take action on the findings of the committee and the commission. Every time we hear the political rhetoric that action would be initiated to book the guilty. So far none has been booked as the State is being soft. From Pratapsingh Kairon to Bofors including J. Jayalalitha, We have found many paradoxes.

Pratapsingh Kairon was one of the best chief ministers during the period of Nehru as he laid the foundation for a prosperous Punjab. But allegations were brought against him. Likewise Tamil Nadu has been adjudged as the first State in implementing social welfare programmes and considered as the best pro-poor State according to the 10th Finance Commission. Certificate of excellence was awarded to the concerned Minister and she was booked within a couple of months as she was involved in large scale corruption when she held the same portfolio of social welfare. How do we conceptualise these paradoxes? Offices of the President and Prime Minister are not exceptions. Leakage of information to foreign agencies has been traced and some of the officials have been dropped from the key positions and yet the same officials have got higher positions later, and how this happened in the system when it functions within the framework of rules and regulations.

Wards of ministers, secretaries, executives of business houses are pursuing their educational programmes in the western countries by investing a huge sum of money with the belief that western institutions are known for quality. How it was possible for them to send their wards to western countries for their studies with huge amount of investment? After retirement, secretaries of many departments take assignment in foreign countries and serve them for many years to the satisfaction of the concerned business houses. How is it possible for them to get such higher positions in the business houses of the western countries? — is a big question.

These are some of the issues I quote just to indicate the paradoxes in the Indian political and administrative system. This needs a total review and proper conceptualization. This has been time and again indicated by two eminent intellectuals, namely, M.N. Srinivas and Rajni Kothari in their speeches and writings. They also indicated that the evolution of such a framework to study corruption should be based on the moral ethos of our country and not on the framework given by the funding agencies of the West. Thus the need of the hour is proper conceptualization.

B. EXPERIENCE

Introduction

Corruption has come to stay as a factor in polity, society and administration. As a result studies have been conducted and ranking has been made among the countries. Public appeal and plea have been made to contain corruption. New concepts like good governance, transparent administration, accountability in governance, empowering people have gained currency among the academics for deep probing and analysis. The funding institutions are funding for development with warnings to the countries concerned that unless steps are taken to reduce corruption, funding projects will be reviewed and that if need arises funding would be stopped. This alarm has perturbed the leaders of the government to make some demonstrations that the government is alert about it and is taking steps to contain it. Transactions are on in this regard and yet whether the misery of the poor is reduced is a major question. To talk on the subject and to analyse the ramifications of corruption individuals and organisations are many but which is the institution and who is the individual who can contain it? — This question has been thought over by a department of study (Political Science and Development Administration) in a University (Gandhigram Rural Institute — Deemed University). Hence, this exercise.

The Problem

Corruption is not new to Indian soil and it had been in practice from the dawn of modern civilization as it differentiates moral code from legal code. Modern civilization classified the activities of the society, government, individual and developed framework to govern the activities. Hence institutions had been devised even during the monarchical days. It has been systematically devised in the modern democracy by creating institutions to check corruption. Despite all these steps corruption has established its tentacles in every sphere of human activities to the extent of eating away the vitals of the Indian social ethos. In the society, sections which have got linkages with the government somehow or other manage themselves without much difficulty. But the poor have to suffer and they are in the clutches of the corrupt coterie. Much has been said about corruption but very little has been done to contain it in practice. Hence instead of talking and deliberating, some initiatives could be taken at the micro level and the same can be a model for expansion also and therefore, this exercise is initiated.

The Exercise

To move from the domain of knowledge to action, an area has been chosen and an individual has been selected. Vadugampadi, a village panchayat, and its president Mr. Perumal have been chosen for this onerous task. Vadugambadi is a service village of the Department of Political Science and Development Administration and hence it is felt that this exercise could be done here. It is a considered opinion of all that corruption could be contained and eliminated only by the joint venture of the people and the government. Moreover corruption is not a one-way process but a two-way process. Corruption is not only demanding but also inducing to demand and to patronise the practice. To curb this two-way practice it is felt that it is necessary to evolve institutional mechanism and to involve the people as community to contain corruption.

Mr. Perumal, a young and committed Gram Panchayat President with a communist background, came forward to perform this exercise in his panchayat as he commands respect and regard for his transparent activities in the panchayat among the people. It is a panchayat reserved for

SC and he got elected in a contest with the support of all communities. It is strange to note that he is recognised by all caste leaders in the panchayat and hence this panchayat has been selected for this venture.

All caste leaders from the Vadugampadi panchayat with the elected members of the wards of the panchayat including the president and vice-president were invited for a preparatory meet in Gandhigram Rural Institute. Adventuristically nearabout eighty members have participated in the preparatory meeting. Since objectives of the meet were clear, the meeting did not take much time for briefing. With introductory remarks of the Vice-Chancellor of the Institute groups have been formed to indicate the sufferings of the people in the rural areas due to corrupt practices prevalent in the governance and to suggest remedies and solutions to protect the people from this evil practice. First group indicated the aspects in which corrupt practices are prevalent which ultimately affect the rustic folk. They are :

1. Revenue Department and especially the officials, namely, Tahsildar, Revenue Inspector and Village Administrative Officers are corrupt bullies demanding money for each and every certificate people demand from them, whether it is income certificate or community certificate or heir certificate. When they seek any certificate, without giving money they cannot get the same. For every certificate there is a fixed price. As the people know of this practice, however poor they may be, they have to prepare themselves to pay the amount to get things done. Yet another area for money making for the Revenue Department is issuing of ration card. Even for genuine cases, they demand money. From the entire village no one has obtained the card without giving money to the concerned officials. Extra cards have been given to many individuals after getting money from them. Thus it is a money-spinning exercise for the revenue officials.
2. Police stations are institutions to trigger conflict

among individuals and groups and to settle the same they demand money from both the groups and individuals. Police stations have brokers for mediation. Poor people in the village do not know how to approach police station to settle dispute. As long as it was confined to village itself it was not a problem. If somebody goes to the police station that is the beginning of the exercise to invite police into the village. Police have used the ignorance of the people for their advantage and finally nobody gains out of the interference of the police in the settlement of disputes. The peaceful atmosphere of the village has been disturbed because of the police intervention.

3. Block Development Office and its officials are corrupt to the core. They demand money individually and collectively from the individual beneficiary and the entire village for the benefits they provide through the schemes and programmes. Here also organised brokers are functioning. They have fixed rates for each and every scheme. Likewise Indira Awas Yojna, IRDP and other programmes have been started by the government but the people do not know how to apply and what are the eligibility conditions to get the benefits and hence their ignorance has been conveniently exploited by the brokers. Moreover, the schemes and their details are not in print for wider circulation. People do not know how to apply and to whom should they apply. From attender to Development Officer, commission money has to be shared. Even after the installation of the elected panchayats in position of power the officials demand the same without any fear. Thus corruption has become an accepted phenomenon in administering development.
4. Ration shop is yet another area where large-scale corruption takes place by which the entitlement of the poor is denied. First the essential commodities are not distributed for all the needy families. Influential individuals in the villages draw the

rations of many families. Sometimes they are sold in the private markets. Further even if the articles are distributed to card-holders, the weights and measures are not correct. Poor men's quota has been enjoyed by the rich in the villages.

5. Natural resources of the rural areas have been exploited by the rich for their own advantage and in this government has been helpful and officials have been supportive. Natural resources are the entitlements of the people who live in the area irrespective of their status.

The second group has suggested the following measures:

> The group went deep into the domains of both aspects, namely, beneficiaries and adversaries. Corruption is not only due to the taker alone and it is due to giver also. To reduce or to end corruption, both should take place simultaneously, namely, giver should stop giving bribe and taker should stop taking bribe. Where to begin — is the question. They themselves admitted that on most of the occasions givers for their own advantage propelled the takers to accept this kind of offers as they were getting undue benefits. Having trained in getting bribe, they continue to demand bribe from all. Initiation should come from the givers that they won't give bribe for getting things done illegally. When there is no giver for unlawful things there won't be any pressure for the taker. Further there should be organised activities for resistance to the corrupt practices. It should be a mass-based one. When there is a case of corruption in any governmental organisation it has to be opposed collectively with the support of the masses.

Based on the argument presented by themselves, they have resolved to make a publicity openly through various means that Vadugampadi panchayat is a corruption-free village which will not give bribe for getting things done.

First they have resolved to constitute a people's committee with the support of the panchayat to ensure intervention wherever the problems of corruption creep in Vadugampadi village. Whenever cases of corruption are reported with much resistance from the corrupt bullies, an organised attempt has to be made. As a first step they have decided to erect a very big board at the entrance of the village with the words "Vadugampadi corruption-free village people's panchayat". Further it has to be published in popular newspapers that the whole village has resolved to fight corruption. Thus steps have been taken to contain corruption at the micro level. It can be a model for other panchayats to follow.

12
Capacitization for Local Governance

73rd Constitutional Amendment Act and the subsequent enactment of the State Local Bodies Act of 1994 provide a large number of responsibilities to the local body leaders. To discharge all those responsibilities in a highly fragmented communities and complicate administrative system the local body leaders need adequate skill and capacity. Of all the prerequisites for smooth functioning of local bodies to deliver goods, capacity-building exercise for local body leaders is foremost and imperative. It has been indicated in many fora that the leaders or representatives recruited for different authoritative bodies, namely, national parliament and State legislatures should have adequate skill and capacity to perform their role and function in a fast changing socio-political and economic system and therefore their training is an imperative need. But nobody took keen interest in it. As a consequence our parliamentary institutions are fastly deteriorating in their standard of performance. The local body institutions cannot and should not follow the beaten path of the higher level representative institutions as these bodies are closely monitored by the people and the representatives in the local bodies come in close contact of the people every day and they have to be responsive to their calls. Hence a programme of training for Gram Panchayat presidents was conceived by Rajiv Gandhi Chair for Panchayati Raj Studies and the proposal was sent to CAPART Hyderabad for financial support. As Rajiv Gandhi Chair for Panchayati Raj Studies was instrumental in evolving a training module based on the exercise done at national level in Hyderabad for Tamil Nadu Planning Commission, CAPART Hyderabad was kind enough to approve the module and sanction the required financial support to take up the training programme for Gram Panchayat leaders for about five districts. To start with, the exercise has been planned for all Gram Panchayat presidents in two districts, namely, Dindigul and Sivagangai and on experimental basis the same exercise has to be done for women and dalits in three districts, namely, Madurai, Ramanathapuram and Pudukkottai. In the first leg the evolved training module can be tested and accordingly modifications could be effected in the training. This programme was a beginning of a massive exercise. It is being done in batches. Each group consists of forty to forty-five presidents of Gram Panchayats. The training content of the programme includes the historical aspects of the Panchayati Raj System, constitutional aspects of the panchayats, main provisions of the federal and State Acts, planning experience in India for economic growth and development, micro level planning for comprehensive development of the areas, activity dimensions of the panchayats on twenty-nine subjects in the 11th Schedule, behavioural and performance dimensions of the presidents of the Gram Panchayats. The methodology of training is based more on dialogue and discussion. Vital issues have been video-taped and shown to them. Field trips have been arranged to model panchayats to demonstrate the success of programmes by the active involvement of the people. Pre- and post-evaluation of the training programme has been done through administering an interview schedule. Information has been collected from the leaders on the practical problems faced by them when they perform their role and function in the panchayats.

Perception of the Leaders on New Panchayati Raj System

Before the commencement of the training exercise a schedule was circulated among the trainees to elicit their perception and understanding of the new Panchayati Raj System. Their perceptions are explained here.

The perception that panchayats are to perform the service functions is lingering in the minds of leaders as they are not aware of the provisions and main implications of the New Panchayati Raj System. They had a rough idea about the new system that it would fulfil the basic needs of the people and provide basic amenities to the community. They presumed that more powers would be given to panchayats and equally more amount of money would also be given to panchayats. This impression has been created among the people by the media. They said that they could not procure copies of the 73rd amendment to the Constitution of India and hence they did not read the provisions of the Act. They did not care to read the provisions of the Tamil Nadu Panchayati Act of 1994 even though it was supplied to the Gram Panchayat leaders as the entire act is in a language which is not understandable to them despite the fact that it is in Tamil. Even the candidates who have contested the election, did not believe that the election would be conducted when the Act was enacted. Likewise they had a notion that the political parties will not evince interest in conducting the election. The moment election was announced, they joined the fray with the hope to enjoy more powers and resources as MPs and MLAs. They have openly admitted that they have spent money for electioneering ranging between rupees thirty-five thousand to two lakhs.

In the pretest schedule, there are about twelve questions. They are:

(a) basic objectives of the new panchayati raj system;
(b) special features of the new system;
(c) functions of the new panchayati raj system;
(d) responsibilities of the presidents of gram panchayat;
(e) ways and means to perform their role successfully;
(f) methodology of organising the people and to involve them in the development process;
(g) possibilities for rural economic development;
(h) people's participation in panchayati activities;
(i) women's development;
(j) SC/ST development activities;
(k) social justice; and
(l) the characteristics of a good leader in the panchayat.

Their responses to the above questions are as follows:

(a) panchayat is to elicit their basic needs;
(b) panchayat is to fulfil the basic needs;
(c) panchayat is to implement the government schemes for the poor;
(d) panchayat is to provide basic facilities in the rural areas;
(e) panchayat has three-tier panchayati system;
(f) panchayat will be a permanent entity;
(g) panchayat will have 29 subjects in 11th Schedule;
(h) panchayat will have a gram sabha;
(i) panchayat is to select beneficiaries for government schemes;
(j) panchayat is to supervise fair price shop;
(k) panchayat is to mobilise resources for panchayats;
(l) panchayat is to construct culverts, bridges houses for the poor;
(m) panchayat is to lay roads, and dig wells;
(n) panchayat is to maintain sanitation;
(o) panchayat is to protect the environment;
(p) panchayat is to do afforestation activities;
(q) panchayat is to protect the common property resources;
(r) panchayat is to take steps for development of women;
(s) panchayat is to convene the panchayat meetings periodically; and
(t) panchayat is to organise gram sabha meetings periodically.

The presidents of gram panchayats are having a rough idea about what the new panchayats have to perform. They again and again reiterate the service functions as the functions of the panchayats. They forget about the original functions of the local bodies as per the provisions of the Act. They are not well aware of the basic objective of the 73rd Constitutional Amendment. They have not mentioned about the economic development activities and social justice. During the past one and a half years, the gram panchayat presidents have been oriented by the officials to implement schemes and programmes of the federal and State governments. Hence their mind-set is that the gram panchayat leaders are to implement schemes and programmes of the State and Central governments. Even in discussion they ask more questions about schemes. They are not much worried about the planning, and resource mobilization for economic activities.

Problems that Gram Panchayat Presidents Face in the Field

Group discussions are being arranged to elicit the problems which they face in the field while performing their role and function. Their problems are presented here.

1. Presidents of gram panchayats are not aware of all the rural development programmes and schemes. They know of only a few programmes from the officials.
2. Needs of the people are going on increasing which need enormous amount of resources to meet them. To meet all their requirements there is no plan.
3. Employees and teachers working within the purview of panchayats, are not employees of panchayats and they are all employees of the Government and hence the employees are not accountable to the local bodies; as a result schools are not properly managed. Yet the presidents are to set right the primary schools in the villages.
4. Resources (both in the form of money mobilised from within and drawn from panchayati union and DRDA for schemes) are inadequate to meet the demands.
5. Capacity of the workers working in the rural areas is inadequate to meet the probiems in the rural society. Repair works are not done in time and the technicians cause inordinate delay. Rates for the repairing work are very low and hence nobody turns towards these works. For the purchase of materials for the repairing works or replacement, presidents have no option but to give more money than the market rate.
6. Providing shelter is a major problem in the rural

areas. Whether it is providing patta or housing facility presidents have to face lot of problems as needs are more and available resources are limited. Moreover while providing these facilities discretion of officials plays an important role rather than the rules of the programmes and schemes.

7. IRDP beneficiary selection is a major problem due to the interference of the politicians, MLAs and MPs.
8. It is very difficult to get the village map from the revenue department. There is absolutely no cooperation from the department in this regard.
9. It is very difficult to remove encroachment from the common properties. It requires the cooperation of Revenue Department and police. Absolutely they are not cooperating with the Gram Panchayats.
10. Common property resources have not been maintained well to yield income to panchayats since they are not under the control of the local bodies.
11. Needs are unmet even after the panchayats have come into being.
12. There is no relationship between the needs and the schemes.
13. Administrative procedures at the lower level are still complicated.
14. It is difficult to provide employment opportunities to the needy.
15. Officials domination over the elected leaders is evident and they dictate terms to the leaders.
16. People's mind-set is that everything has to be done by the government. People are only to receive. They expect each and everything to be taken care of by the local body leaders.
17. Common property resource management should be given to local bodies. Sand quarry and other natural resources are the properties of the community. But now by a single order they are taken away from the people without getting the consent of the community.
18. Powers of the Union Engineer are unlimited and UE is the embodiment of corruption. He is more powerful than the Block Development Officer. He is the person

responsible for clearing bills, proposals and hence he makes the Gram Panchayat presidents to dance to his tune. Union Engineer demands 15% commission for each and every work.

19. Interference of MPs and MLAs in the affairs of local bodies is increasing and their words are respected and their interference in the local body affairs disturbs the activities of the local bodies. Increasing the amount for MLAs and MPs would be an attempt to thwart the local bodies.
20. In all government functions organised in the rural areas, the concerned constituency MP and MLA are invited but the local body leaders are not respected and invited.
21. Presidents are elected by the people and vice-presidents of Gram Panchayats are elected by ward members. But the vice-president is also required to sign the cheque. It disturbs the atmosphere and administration.
22. Women presidents are not respected by the officials. Sometimes they are ill treated in the offices. They face lot of problems in the offices of the government.
23. More flexibility should be given in the schemes to local body leaders to meet the basic needs of the people.
24. Public distribution system should be supervised by the panchayats in the local areas.
25. Government orders are not properly circulated among the local body leaders.
26. For each and every transaction officials in the panchayat union demand money openly.
27. There is no linkage between panchayat and the cooperatives.
28. Makkal Nala Paniyalargal are in the panchayats and they have to work under panchayats and they have to get their salary from panchayats. Yet, in practice they are not working in coordination with the president. Hence the procedure of giving salary to them in panchayat union office should be stopped.
29. Ration cards are to be distributed through Gram

Sabha to eliminate bogus cards.

30. For making estimate and settlement of bills, officials take lot of time but to execute the programmes and schemes officials give short time to leaders. This has to be avoided.
31. Birth certificate, death certificate, community certificate should be issued by the panchayats through a resolution. Erring leaders have to be punished.
32. There is no linkage between the revenue department and the development departments.
33. The role of District Panchayat is not known to Gram Panchayat presidents.
34. MPs, MLAs, District Panchayat Members, Block Panchayat members are operating funds to execute certain works in the villages without the knowledge of the people and the Gram Panchayats. All these works are to be integrated. These works are not related to needs and hence lot of money is being wasted by allotting them for execution.
35. Panchayats are advised to take up works without claiming any advance. Where can they find money for work. Even after completing the work the presidents have to move from pillar to post to get the money from the offices and for which they have to give bribe to officials at all levels.
36. Allocation of money to MP, MLA, District Panchayat Member, Block Panchayat Member tempts the Village Panchayat Ward Members also to ask for some amount of money for works.

Their Perception after Training

Before the valedictory session, again an interview schedule was distributed to elicit their opinion about the implications of training. Apart for filling up the schedule, they openly express their opinion about the training programme in the valedictory session. Some VIP will be there in each programme to distribute the certificate. This valedictory session has an advantage for the trainers to correct themselves in their methodology of training. Their perceptions about the Panchayati Raj after the training programme have been compiled and presented below.

1. They perceived the long-term implications of the new Panchayati Raj system.
2. The mind-set that local bodies are to execute schemes and programmes of the governments has been changed and the new mind-set that local bodies are to work for economic development and social justice has been created.
3. They learnt to make the panchayats as people's panchayats and not the government's panchayats.
4. It is not power but it is only responsibility that makes the panchayats a self-governing institution.
5. They realise that without money panchayats can do many programmes in the villages.
6. They realise the original functions of the local bodies.
7. They feel that they are change agents.
8. Key provisions of the 73rd constitutional Amendment Act and Tamil Nadu Panchayati Raj Act are known to the Gram Panchayat presidents.
9. How to prepare perspective plan for rural development is known to them.
10. It is recognised as a governing institution.
11. Schemes and programmes of the government are known to them.
12. Role and responsibilities of the presidents are known to them.
13. How to create employment opportunities in the villages by making use of the available skills is known to them.
14. How to mobilize resources in the rural areas is known to them.
15. How to make the panchayats as movement of the people is known to them.
16. How to get the government orders from the officials is known to them.
17. How to get the works done in the government offices

is known to them.

18. How to conduct the panchayat administration in a transparent way is known to them.
19. How to mobilize people and to involve them in the panchayat activities is known to them.
20. Issues and solutions are known to them.
21. How to protect the environment is known to them.
22. How to make the rural areas 'green' is known to them.

Conclusion

The capacity building exercise for Gram Panchayat presidents has to go a long way to achieve its results. It is a good beginning by which their mind-set has been changed. Lot of information has been exchanged. Their potentiality has been drawn out. 60% of attendance has been ensured despite the instruction from the government. Material supplied to them is properly used by the participants of the training programme. Women are more enthusiastic than men. One aspect is obvious from their interactions i.e., they need a supporting base as government is not favourable to them.

13
People's Planning Exercise in a Gram Panchayat

Venus	:	Vadugampadi Panchayat school in Puliyampatti village
Date	:	01-08-89 (Saturday)
Time	:	10.30 AM to 3.30 PM
Participants	:	President, Vice-President, Ward Members, Planning Committee Members along with the people drawn from each hamlet.
Invitees	:	Vice-Chancellor from Gandhigram Rural Institute, Team of Staff from Rajiv Gandhi Chair for Panchayati Raj Studies;

Team of Staff drawn from various departments of Gandhigram Rural Institute.

Methodology: Informing the mechanics of the exercise to the participants;

Introducing the planning framework by the experts; participants need assessment exercise; Experts' opinion on the issues; Consolidation of the report on the needs of the people.

Priority Needs

1. Need of link road to the hamlets.
2. Need of employment opportunities to women both literate and illiterate.
3. Need of employment opportunities to youth (both literate and illiterate).
4. Need of a High School for their wards.

5. Skill-oriented education to their women.
6. Need of road facility from Kovilur to Subramaniyapuram.
7. Need of library facility.
8. Need of village information centre.
9. Poramboke land has to be used profitably.
10. Necd of clean and calm atmosphere in the premises of the school.
11. Need of water facility to the schools in the panchayat.
12. Need of remedial action to set right the noon meal centre in the schools.
13. Need of Kalathumadu for agricultural purposes.
14. Ration has to be regulated through the public distribution system.
15. Bogus ration cards have to be removed.
16. Speed-breaker to be put on the main road to avoid accidents.
17. Need of drinking water supply to Narimedu village.
18. Need of street light facility to Narimedu.
19. Housing patta has to be given to the people who are in the Poramboke settlement of Kulathur.
20. There is a small dam very near to the village which will provide water to 200 acres of land for cultivation. But now due to the leakage in the shutter water is being wasted. Repair has to be done immediately.
21. Approach road to the dam has to be repaired.
22. Awareness has to be created about sanitation.
23. Need of toilet facilities to all the hamlets.
24. Wherever toilets are provided by NGO they are to be used, and for which steps have to be taken.
25. Most of the men are having the habit of consuming alcohol. This has to be arrested. Prohibition committee has to be formed to create awareness about the implications of drugs and alcohol.
26. Need of housing facility to the SC/ST in all the hamlets.
27. VAO is demanding money for each and every certificate he is issuing to the people.
28. 100 acres forest land has to be fruitfully utilised for

growing trees.

29. Women's organisation is needed.
30. To settle petty quarrels and disputes among the people, an empowered people's committee has to be constituted.
31. Need of burial ground and its approach road with lighting facilities.

Interventions

As the people are oriented to think on the lines of the government schemes, they have been always talking about the demands in the pattern of the programmes of the government. Their demands centre around housing patta, construction of houses, drinking water facilities, street light, educational facilities, medical facilities and employment opportunities. They were unable to think beyond all those demands. Against this background, the academics intervened and said that the planning exercise is not for getting the schemes from the government but to plan for holistic development of the village. To make the development of the panchayat as sustainable development, the people should be provided with basic facilities and opportunities should be provided to them decide their destiny. Hence this exercise should have long-range implications. Academics indicated the problems in the villages of Vadugampadi such as :

— insanitation in the village,
— unprotected water supply,
— improper management of schools,
— improper management of the facilities that are available,
— common property resources are not properly managed,
— Lack of awareness on the part of the people about child care,
— village full of unmanaged dust and waste,
— unconcern about health care, and
— unutilised skills of the people in the villages.

After indicating the problems by the people and the interventions of the academics, it was decided that various committees have to be formed to collect vital statistics about the issues and based on the data planning exercise would be done in small groups by inviting experts from outside.

The following committees have been formed:

(a) Health Committee,
(b) Education Committee,
(c) Peace Committee,
(d) Common Property Resource Management Committee, and
(e) Committee for Employment Generation.

All the committees have been entrusted with the responsibility of collecting data through the participatory rural appraisal method. Based on the data proposals have to be formulated and the formulated proposals have to be reviewed in a seminar.

One noticeable feature in the whole exercise is that the people who participated in the discussions have not only projected the problems but also suggested solutions. While going through the demands and the solutions, one would observe that there is no much difficulty in solving those problems. They are within the reach of the people. Most of the problems require only a change in the mind-set of the people. A large-scale awareness creation on various aspects of living conditions such as environment, sanitation, protected water consumption, hygiene nutritive food intake, menace of drugs, harnessing natural resources and skills for productivity would make the village a self-sufficient village in every respect at present. The whole exercise depends on the continuous participation of the people in the planning process and development process of the village in the days to come.

Villages in the Vadugampadi Gram Panchayat

1. Seelamanayakkan Kulathur
2. Othaiyur
3. Angankulam

4. Ponnikulam
5. Siruthangal
6. Nallinagar
7. Pannapatti
8. Indira Nagar
9. Vadakkuthalipatti
10. Naduthalippatti
11. Therkuthalippatti
12. Rajiv Nagar
13. Ramagiri
14. Kombaiyankulam
15. Aranmanaiyur
16. Chokkankulathur
17. Posakkiliapatti
18. Nallasivikapuram
19. Puliyampatti
20 Paraipatti
21. Thoppur
22. Pomnakavundanputhur
23. Merku Vadugampadi
24. Kilakku Vadugampadi
25. Anna Nagar
26. Bharathi Nagar
27. Muthakavundanur
28. Varatharajapuram
29. Gandhi Nagar
30. Koppanayakkanpatti
31. V. Kulathur
32. Narimedu
33. Devakavundanur
34. Chokkalingampillaiyur
35. Subramaniapillaiyur
36. Velayuthakkavundanur
37. Selvapuram
38. Venkatesapuram

14
Food Security and Grassroots Governance

Introduction

The concept of security had drawn the attention of all by equating it exclusively to a military problem and to think of the military problem as being exclusively a weapon system. National security has been a much debated issue for several decades. Keeping the Nation-State intact is the primary objective of the polity today. Moreover, nations have spent huge amounts of money for purchasing arms and ammunition. Public spending on military is much more than the expenditure on social development.[1] National security through militia cannot sustain forever. Piling of more arms and ammunition will bring only insecurity, not security. There are other issues which are so vital and yet they are not much debated among the public. Even then it is a very big question as to what extent a nation can be complacent when millions of people go to bed with hungry stomach. As long as the populace have faith in fatalism, the State can be complacent with its existing structural arrangement. The moment people realise the role and responsibility of the State and government, they will claim their rights and entitlements.[2]

The ongoing conflict among collectivities within Nation-States demonstrates the conscious efforts of the groups in demanding their due. The rise of more number of groups with package of demands as entitlements will directly question the credibility of the political system and thereby governance will be at stake. Military equipment will bring security to the territory of a sovereign Nation-State but it will not bring security to the people, Society and government. Fulfilling the entitlements through a rationalistic policy options will bring security to the society and government. Of the entitlements such as education, sanitation, employment, water, and others, food is essential and vital which decides the quality of the people in the society and government. Hence food security draws the attention of the policy-makers of late and it has been discussed widely from the fora of international standing to panchayati level as to what extent food could be secured to the people sustainably.

Global Initiatives

Robert S. McNamara, the then president of the World Bank while delivering an address at MIT on world change and world security, emphatically stressed the need for a fresh thinking on the concept of security from the perspective of military security of a nation to world security in the backdrop of alleviating human miseries through governance by identifying the vital issues affecting the people due to population growth.[3] The intellectuals who have concentrated their attention on war, revolution, conflict and their impact and consequences[4] in the society have shifted their emphasis from death due to conflict to death due to hunger. Efforts are on from international level and yet conditions are not changed. In 1974, the World Food Conference in Rome resolved that by 1984 no child, woman or man should go to bed hungry and no human being physical or mental potential should be stunted by malnutrition. Even after twenty-two years of the passing of the resolution we see 700 million people go to bed with hungry stomach and 800 million people suffer from chronic under-nutrition in less developed countries and 200 million people suffer from malnutrition in the low income food deficient countries. The World Bank has brought out a gloomy picture about the creation of a hunger-free world by estimating that 1080 million people are totally living in sub-human conditions. They cannot afford enough food and they are affected by growth disorders.[5] Of the 1080 million 900 million people are in absolute poverty. Every year 13.5 million children below the age of five die in less developed countries because of malnutrition. FAO took initiative to look into the issues through the world summit. On the other hand the new economic policy initiated through economic reform touched the vital aspects of food security. GATT and WTO totally removed the barriers in the flow of the food material from one place to another without any restriction. In the world with vast gap between the rich and poor nations, the liberalization of agriculture would mean only liberalising the trade in agricultural commodities, not liberalising agriculture and liberating producers. Hence there are two trends in food security system.[6] One is with altruistic perception and another one is based on maximizing market efficiency in food production.

It is heartening to note that a ten-point declaration was made in Chennai with the initiative of M.S. Swaminathan Foundation in collaboration with intellectuals of many countries. In the Chennai declaration the concept of food security has been totally redefined. It is not mere supply of food to the needy. It is more than that when the concept of food security gained currency. In the 1970s, it was perceived as mere supply of food to the needy and that it needed only increasing agricultural production and proper distribution. It was believed that it is only production and distribution. Over the years the dimensions of food security have been expanded and enlarged. Thus, concept of food security has been changed into livelihood security. Thus, food security as conceptualized in this study is livelihood security for the households and the members thereof which ensures both physical and economic access to balanced diet, safe drinking water, environmental sanitation, primary education and basic health care.[7] Thus production of agriculture has to be increased, distribution mechanism has to be perfected, health care system has to be properly managed local body initiative to protect the environment has to be encouraged. The narrowed down concept has been expanded dimensionally.

Indian Context

It is very clear in the Constitution that food security is a fundamental right and it is an entitlement. Article 47 unequivocally states that "the State shall regard the raising of the level of nutrition and the standard of living of its people and the improvement of public health as among its primary duties".[8] Food security is a major aspect of governance in India from 1939 onwards. In 1939 rationing was started in Bombay. It was further enlarged after the Bengal famine of 1943. After Independence government retained the power of imports and distribution. Domestic procurement was also encouraged, food zones were created, restrictions on movement of foodgrains and compulsory levies were imposed and private trade was banned. Production was encouraged by creating Agricultural Price Commission and Food Corporation of India in the year 1965. One of the prime objectives of the FCI is to feed the supply lines of the public distribution system so that grains can be distributed at reasonable prices especially to the weaker sections of society. Our macro distributive system and its linkages with micro distributive system have not solved the very basic issue of hunger.[9]

It is not so easy to procure the needed food materials and stock them safely and distribute them to the needy people. It needs a very comprehensive policy options of the government. Increasing the agricultural production, procuring them by giving reasonable prices to the farmers, stock them safely and distribute them to the poor at fair price. It is all the more important to make the people to buy them. Unless a conducive climate is not created the distributed food will not create any impact on the output of the people. Thus enabling individuals to get needed energy to lead a human life is the security ensured through food security.[10] To ensure food security more steps have to be taken at the lower levels of governing institutions. But the activities of the State government will have more linkages with policy options of the federal government. Once it was believed that by increasing food production and controlling population growth food can be secured to everyone in the society. But the policy-makers realised later that only by proper stocking and distributing the stocked food material through a system will ensure food to every individual.

Even after establishing Food Corporation of India and public distribution system they could not ensure food security to the people. The question is what for food? What type of food? Will it give needed energy to the people for their work and under what circumstances the food provided to the individuals will provide needed energy to them? — are the major questions to be raised at present as the concept has been redefined. To achieve this two-pronged action is an imperative, namely, micro-action and macro-action. Macro-action deals with policy environment which includes enacting a Food Security Act, pricing agricultural commodities, creation of employment opportunities, creating an effective public distribution system, rational use of water and land preventing erosion of these finite resources, devising a grain saving livestock policy to improve the availability of animal products, evolving a coastal aqua-culture policy for sustainable utilization of the coastal system.

Micro action includes integrating the provision of safe drinking water, basic sanitation, housing and elementary education, achieving mass literacy by making school education compulsory and by abolishing child labour, providing employment opportunity based on their skills, strengthening public distribution system, administering social justice, improving the cooperative sector to support agriculture and village industries for both production and marketing and a number of other actions. Thus an appropriate policy package has to be initiated in the given environment and accordingly structural arrangements either to create or to modify the existing institutions and to empower the people with needed information to make use of the policies programmes and to handle the institutional arrangements for the betterment of the people.[11]

What Ails Our System?

To increase production in agricultural sector, the government should have an apt policy option and equally the farmers should have the capacity to make use of the policy options. Secondly, the people should have the ability to handle the appropriate institutions to implement the policies. Wherever we find linkages there one would find success and good performance. In India, we feel that there is a vast gap between the people and the government and hence government is repeatedly exploited by the select citizens who are having the capacity to understand the process of governance.[12] At present schemes and programmes are numerous for rural development and proper utilization of all the schemes and programmes would bring a sea-change in the society. But we are not witnessing the expected changes as the schemes and programmes of the people are not properly perceived and utilized by the people.[13] Most of the occasions they do not know the value of the programmes and their implications. Major part of the works has to be done at the micro level through the people's organisation—Panchayati Raj.

What a Panchayat Can Do?

Panchayati Raj has been perceived properly by the people and it is an institution of the people and not the government. These institutions are to harness the powers and potentiality of the people. It has such a flexibility to give wider opportunity to the people to take responsibility to manage their own affairs. A panchayat can provide safe drinking water supply, maintain basic sanitation, protect the environment, provide elementary education and housing create enough employment opportunities to the rural people by making use of their skills. By creating a green cover in the villages, employment opportunities could be created. Agro-based industries have to be organised and people can be employed in those industries. To control the explosion of population community can initiate the action plan by which an enabling environment has to be created where children are born by choice. To administer social justice protective discrimination and affirmative action could be taken at the grassroots level in utilising the government programmes and schemes. Thus all activities could be initiated from the perspective of the resources, not from the perspective of the market. Pro-nature activities will alone bring equity and justice to the people through the local institutions.[14]

Experience in Tradition

Our traditional and conventional belief system in our academic pursuits refuses to take the principles which emerge from the tradition for the management of natural resources and common properties. For land utilization and water management we had best management principles and they had been adopted by the communities through the organisations where one would find rational and equitable utilization of resources for the benefits of the households. Effectively and actively people participated in the management of the resources. Resources which had been considered as vital for agricultural activities, had been carefully managed by the community.[15] Though the organisations were dominated by socially recognised upper class, social justice was done and equity was administered. In the same way food bank had been operated in many villages in 1950s and 1960s and even today. Food bank experience was very rewarding because equitable distribution could be made thereby.[16] Now fair price shops are available in the rural areas and are being operated by the Department of Civil Supply of the Government of Tamil Nadu. It is a major area where everyone is concentrating and sometimes the modalities of the functioning of the fair price shops decide the electoral victory of the party or parties. A vital element of corruption disrupts the very functioning of the fair price shops which deprives certain individuals of their entitlements. The major demand of the people in the rural area is regulating the fair price shop to enable it to provide essential food material to all the ration-card holders and especially the poor.[17]

Integrated policy initiatives of the federal government coupled with the creation of institutions to operationalise the policies and programmes by the State would result in delivering the goods to the people. To achieve better results, it is necessary to provide the people with adequate information. As we have seen many failures and pitfalls in the higher level activities at the federal and State level, it is imperative that steps are taken from below. At the grassroots level people are to be mobilised, educated and provided with necessary information to look after their affairs on their own without depending much on outside agencies and especially the government. People have to take up the responsibility of providing essential services for livelihood security. It is, no doubt, a cumbersome process to develop human resources. Human resource development ultimately will enhance the capacity of the people and thereby social development could be achieved. Economic growth need not necessarily be a factor for social development. Wherever the people and their organisations are aware and powerful, social development has been achieved. For achieving social development micro actions are imperative and there too people's participation is a *sine qua non.*[18]

Conclusion

Food security as an inclusive concept deals with many entitlements of the people to have livelihood security. At present mere production and distribution will not ensure safe livelihood. To achieve livelihood security actions have to be taken at different levels. Federal and State governments have to initiate policy options and create needed infrastructural facilities to carry out the programmes and schemes. At the grassroots level representatives and the people have to be vigilant and active in controlling the government machinery, Further their capacity has to be enhanced. People and the leaders at micro level have to evolve devices to have control over the distributive mechanism. By doing so people have more responsibilities and government machineries have less structures and powers. Pro-nature activities have to be initiated and every human activity is to be looked at from the perspective of the resources

Notes and References

1. Ruth Leger Sivard, *World Military and Social Expenditure 1991*, Washington D.C. : World Priorities, 1991, p. 5.
2. Bread for the World Institute, *Hunger 1994: Transforming the Politics of Hunger*, MD USA: Bread for the World Institute, 1993.
3. Robert S. McNamara, *Address to the Massachusetts Institute of Technology*, Cambridge: Massachusetts, 1977.
4. To analyse the ethnic group conflict and the group activities more than one hundred and thirteen institutions have been organised. An array of periodicals have been published. For more details see G. Palanithurai, *Polyethnicity in India and Canada*, New Delhi : MD Publications, 1997.
5. Asha Krishnakumar, " Eradicating hunger: The quest for a food secure world" *Frontline* (November 15, 1996).
6. Vandana Siva, "The Problem" *Seminar*, 433 (September, 1995).
7. UNDP and MSSRF, *Agenda for a Food Secure Asia-Pacific Region by 2010 AD*, Madras: M.S. Swaminathan Research Foundation, 1994. p. xv.
8. *The Constitution of India*, p. 14.
9. Ashok Gulati "Changing Gears", *Seminar*, 433 (September, 1995), pp. 16-17.
10. M.S. Swaminathan and K.N.N.S. Nair, *New Paradigm of Agricultural Research for Sustainable Food Security in the Asia Pacific Region*, Madras: M.S Swaminathan Research Foundation, 1994.
11. M.S.Swaminathan, "Pathway to rural prosperity", *The Hindu Survey of Indian Agriculture 1997*, Madras: The Hindu Publication, 1997.
12. G. Palanithurai, *People's Perception of Politics: An Indian Perspective*, New Delhi : Kanishka Publications, 1994.
13. Hari Mohan Mathur, *Administration Development in The Third World: Constraints and Choices*, New Delhi: Sage Publications, 1986.
14. G. Palanithurai, *Empowering People for Prosperity*, New Delhi: Kanishka Publications, 1994.
15. Kanchan Chopra, Gopal K. Kadekodi and M.N. Murty, *Participatory Development : People and Common Property Resources*, New Delhi : Sage Publications, 1990.
16. "Food Security", *Annual Report 1996-97 Agragamee Kashipur*, pp. 36-41.

17. Rajiv Gandhi, *Report of the Training Programme conducted for Gram Panchayati Presidents of Dindigul and Sivaganga District*, Gandhigram: Rajiv Gandhi Chair, 1998.
18. Some of the activities are indicated in the studies conducted by M.S. Swaminathan Foundation, For more details see Signe Lise Dahl, *Sustainable livelihood Security : Case Study in Sivaranthakam Village*, working paper, MADRAS; MSSRF, 1995; M.S. Swaminathan, S. Rajagopal and S. Sharada, *Hunger Free Area Programme*, working paper, Madras: MSSRF, 1996.

15

The Paradox of an Ethnic Movement

Introduction

Indian polity is known for many paradoxes.[1] Theoretical postulates evolved by the western scholars on democratic process have been completely rejected in the Indian socio-political setting when they were tested.[2] Even to spicy intellectuals who have been in the field of research on Indian polity and society for long, transformation process of the Indian society and polity is a problematic area for theorization as they exhibit varieties of deviations. Tamil province had been setting up new trends in the development process of Indian polity.[3] Province building, State autonomy, more powers to State, equal allocation of resources to regions, establishment of social equity and protective discrimination are some of the new trends established by Tamil polity through its collectivities in the name of 'Dravidian Movement'.[4] Of the changes effected in Indian polity social reform through the ethnic movement under the caption of 'Dravidian Movement' occupied a predominant role in the political and social process of the Tamil province and in turn in Indian politics for about four decades very intensively and extensively.[5] This social reconstruction and reformation process has produced a variety of frameworks to explain the ethnic movement in Tamil province.[6] The basic question revolves around the changes that took place in the Dravidian Movement. To what extent these changes fall well within the framework of an ethnic movement is the main question to be answered in this chapter.

The Issue

Dravidian Movement is an umbrella concept which includes many collectivities from south Indian liberal federation to Puthia Tamilagam (a political party) organised by Dr. Krishnaswamy in the eleventh hour of twelfth general election. Dravidian Movement is significantly identified with a basic tenct of rejecting the hierarchical social order evolved by Hindu religion and bringing an identity for social and political action with an approach of modernization and scientific outlook of life modelled on the western society.[7] The movement had anchored in the domain of rationalism for social reconstruction. But the historical process of the movement has brought several puzzles and paradoxes.[8] The latest being heading the party which claims that it has got the lineages of the Dravidian Movement by a Brahmin (J. Jayalalitha) and having successfully managed the party cadre for about ten years forged an electoral alliance with the Bharatiya Janata Party known for its *Hindutva*, the AIADMK has pushed the academics to look back the theoretical propositions evolved on Dravidian Movement and to review them contextually to explain the new paradox in terms of the changes in identity formation.

Framework to explain the New Paradox

Till the arrival of the western social anthropologists and political sociologists, native scholars had not embarked in the new domain for conceptualisation as the Dravidian Movement has been considered as an aberration of Indian politics and has not been viewed as a phenomenon at all.[9] The school on nationalist paradigm has provided space to look at the issues from the perspective of the federal government[10] and polity, not from the provincial polity and society as they have been considered as insignificant in terms of their contribution in changing the perspective of Indian polity and government. 1967 Election had opened a new chapter in Indian politics which drew the attention of the academics to look at the new phenomenon.[11] Even at this juncture Indian academics especially native scholars have not dared to make any attempt to conceptualise the whole transformation process excepting Iqbal Narain.[12]

The western political sociologists and social anthropologists with liberal funding of the aid agencies have started making inquiries into these issues which could not have been explained through the framework evolved to study Indian politics and hence they tried to conceptualise this movement under the rubric of ethnicity. This process of conceptualization of the Dravidian Movement has helped the movement substantially to expand the bases of its operation. Having set the road for research investigation by the western scholars the native scholars moved into the same domain and track by taking up the evolved propositions and hypotheses for testing repeatedly.[13] Excepting the classical Marxist and neo-Marxist[14] all native scholars had appreciation for the frameworks evolved by the western scholars. The developments in the Dravidian Movement such as the change-over of control over the movement from moneyed non-Brahmin to middle class non-Brahmin, from rational outlook with scientific temper to owing allegiance to primordial institutions and values, from non-Brahminization to non-Congressism, from middle class to lower middle class, from non-Brahminization to Brahminization, from rejection of *Hindutva* to acceptance of *Hindutva* (castist organization) have continuously altered the theoretical premises and in fact the Dravidian Movement is always in transition as the intensity of resistance in accepting the new values by the masses in Tamil society is very less.[15] The changing contours of this movement have brought out a variety of frameworks which do not serve the purpose all the time. From "Primordial loyalty", evolved by Robbert L. Hardgrave Jr., to market-oriented corporate approach of Dravidian Movement evolved by G. Palanithurai,[16] a series of studies have been conducted in the movement and developed a battery of frameworks. Yet those frameworks cannot be of any use in the present circumstances as the new phenomenon is totally different and opposite in nature to the basic values of the Dravidian Movement. Hence a totally fresh attempt has to be made to explain the new phenomenon. This new framework stems from a very basic postulate that people have been trapped in images through the media to achieve a political and social goal for a particular segment of a collectivity.[17] The movement or fluctuation of the collectivity in terms of its activities is primarily determined by the political profit of sharing power to achieve to social goal. To change the contours of the movement pretests have been conducted many times to keep the masses under this trap by projecting the political gains which in turn bring economic benefits. Aligning with Swatantra Party headed by Rajaji by the DMK, taking personal advice from Rajaji by the leader of the DMK E.V. Ramasamy Periyar, aligning with Indian National Congress led by Indira Gandhi by the DMK in 1971 and subsequent alliances with the same party by the DMK and the AIADMK alternatively demonstrated that aligning with national forces for political goal is no way deviant from the main goal of social reconstruction and reformation.[18] Contextually unviable propositions, namely, branding of M.G. Ramachandran as Malayalee and J. Jayalalitha as Brahmin have not gained any support for the Tamil community as the ethnic fervour has gone down to the lowest ebb. Contrarily the slogans like Nehruvin mahale varuka nilayana Atchi tharuka—Daughter of Nehru come, provide stable government after the collapse of Janata government had gained support from the masses. With the support of Tamil Maanila Congress's slogan "Strong India prosperous Tamil Nadu", DMK joined hands with other regional parties to form a government at the centre by leaving the goal of more powers to the province. This has also gained the support of the people.[19] The Tamil Maanila Congress has influenced the DMK to act swiftly in the government sector by altering its policy options. Removal of names of the leaders in the transport corporations and districts is a significant departure from the value premises of the DMK. Likewise withdrawal of reservation of backward classes in the positions of local bodies is yet another event. These changes have brought much acclaim to the DMK Government. Hence any rational discussion to maximize the political gain on any camp will bring the support of the masses. It does not mean the subalterns look at rationally and act in favour of alliances. The subalterns are in the trap of images, namely, Periyar, Anna and M.G.R. To retain the subalterns in the image trap an organised mechanism has been developed and through which messages are given to them in an accepted mode of communication.[20] Party cadres are developed in such a fashion as to get the approval of the masses for all their new proposals and for which cadres are being trained. Thus cadres approval and disapproval plays a decisive role in determining the victory. Major events and incidences have sometimes made the cadres to change their style of functioning. For instance in the 11th general election masses did not allow the AIADMK candidates to visit even their constituencies during electioneering which prevented the cadres performance in the constituency. How cadres take instructions and carry out instructions and on what basis cadres are oriented towards maximizing political profit minimising the loss of the party? Thus the principle of profit works in the decision making process of the cadres. Thus the profit social and economic determines the stability of the party in the masses. With this perspective framework the present political arrangement has to be analysed.

Examination of the Cases

Political alliances in the past three decades have moved out of the ideological contours and remain in the context to capture power by sensitising the masses through emotive issues. Classification of the parties is also very difficult as transition is so fast. In Tamil Nadu there were only two traditions of political parties, namely, national and regional traditions. The Indian National Congress, Socialist Parties, community parties belong to former and the parties which mere considered as offshoot of Dravidar Kazhagam and caste organisations belong to regional tradition. Ideologically speaking the national political parties have taken roots in the process of State formation and nation building and regional political parties have taken roots in the process of province building.[21] For political socialization and political mobilization, issues of the nation had been highlighted with the backdrop of the national struggle for freedom by the national political parties and the regional political parties.

Masses are being socialized and mobilized in the Tamil region by highlighting the regional issues affecting the life of the people in the backdrop of primordial loyalty. In appearance both were working against each other but in reality it was not so. The regional aspirations projected by the regional political parties had been met by the federal government. When the whole of the nation faced crises either during war or any natural calamity regions cooperated and contributed substantially for the unity and integrity of the nation. This is the practice in India for the past fifty years. This symbiotic process had brought success to the regional political parties. The continuing success of these organisations has developed schism both in the national political parties and regional political parties which propelled the political forces to realign themselves to achieve political power.

It is true to our Indian political system that national political parties align with regional political parties and regional political parties align with national political parties to capture power. This tradition of fusion gets the support of the masses as most of the political parties have branched off from the Indian National Congress. Political parties irrespective of their nature whether they are national or regional, use to test their options continuously and in the process they have developed success proposals and on that basis they work in the elections to maximise their profits. Dravidian parties have moved from one domain to another as they met with failure while pursuing the earlier proposals one after another. The Dravidian movement has traversed from atheism to anti-Brahminism, from anti-Brahminism to non-Brahminism from non-Brahminism to anti-north and from anti-north to anti-Congressism and from anti-Congressism to anti-Karunanidhi and anti-MGR and from anti-Karunanidhi to anti-Jayalalitha. In this dialectic and symbiotic process alliances are formed and justified.

Till the formation of an electoral alliance between the AIADMK and the BJP, the political alliances in Tamil Nadu had not moved into the sensitive issue of religion which had not been dragged into the electoral politics. In Tamil Nadu traditionally the Muslim vote banks had been divided into two blocks and in both blocks Dravidian parties were partners of the political alliance. In this twelfth general election with the sound *Hindutva* background BJP aligned with the AIADMK which brings sensations to the onlookers of Tamil Nadu politics. The AIADMK and the BJP combine projects a new proposal which is contradictory in its approaches. Barring the BJP and the Janata Party, all other parties have their Dravidian tint in their approaches. By forging an alliance with the BJP, the BJP's *Hindutva* fervour could be mitigated and the feeling and perception of the people of Tamil Nadu towards the BJP will be changed positively. But the aim of the AIADMK is not to change the perception of the people to mitigate the *Hindutva* fervour of BJP it is only to maximize the winning chance, and to come out from all legal proceedings against J. Jayalalitha as M. Karunanidhi did during the 80's by forging an alliance with the Indian National Congress under the leadership of Indira Gandhi.[22]

Each small group's design in AIADMK - BJP combine is to get at least a seat to retain the cadre for some time. By aligning with the BJP the splinter groups are increasing the possibilities of BJP to establish its hold over the Tamil Province. At the same time the leaders, namely, Subramania Swamy, Vaiko, Dr. Ramdass, K. Ramamoorthy known for their individuality have to keep themselves under the fold of J. Jayalalitha without being vocal in the front even though there are some heart burns in seat sharing exercises.

Had Sonia Gandhi taken this decision of entering into politics earlier, the position of the AIADMK and the DMK-TMC combine would have been different. It would be a tough task for the DMK-TMC combine to emerge victoriously. For the AIADMK the need of the hour is to emerge as a ruling party whether it is with the help of the BJP or the Indian National Congress. It is only to destabilize the ruling DMK party. Because the DMK destabilized the ruling AIADMK party under the leadership of M.G. Ramachandran in 1980 after the Parliament election was over. J. Jayalalitha expects the same to happen if the BJP forms the government at the centre.[23] But in those days it was possible since a single party emerged victorious to form the government at the centre and therefore cases have been dropped against the rival party's government. Today's conditions are set for formation of coalitions. In a coalition arrangement such type of hasty and hazy decisions will destabilize the federal government itself. There is a proof from the Uttar Pradesh incident. Moreover, whenever parliament is weak, office of the president will be very strong.[24] At this juncture president is more powerful than the Prime Ministerial Government. Hence possibility for using Article 356 is very limited as it has been much politicised by the involvement of all political parties. Thus the present political alliances for electoral contest in Tamil Nadu contain inferences which are the fundamental factors which would thwart the very basis of the Dravidian Movement in Tamil Nadu which is inevitable as the limited objectives of the movement have been achieved.[25]

Inferences

The above posited events, explanations and interpretations are lending a few propositions for further testing and validation. Identity of the movement tends to change frequently and fastly to accommodate the changing nature of the expectations of the people. Traditional elements to hold collectivity together have lost their relevance as people are more economically regional. Political alliances are always on the basis of maximising the prospects of electoral victory. Aligning with opposing forces in terms of ideologies is not new. AIADMK has followed the path of the DMK. The DMK was a trend-setter. By making alliance with the Indian National Congress the DMK has initiated the process of assimilation with the mainstream. AIADMK followed the footsteps of the DMK to align with the BJP and by which the basic value premises of the Dravidian Movement have been given a go-by.

The concept of stability was the slogan coined by the DMK for Indian National Congress in 1980. The same slogan has been used by the AIADMK for BJP. Since people are in the image trap, convincing the cadres of the party is so easy because cadres are looking for economic prosperity as businessmen. Thus it was easy for the leaders to switch over to any frontiers which are suitable to maximise their political profit. Possibility of using the ethnic chords like language, culture, non-Brahminism is very remote. Thus attracting the voters by any emotional issues of ethnicity is very difficult. Getting the approval for political parties to reach power from the public is not so easy. This process will be tougher in the years to come. Tamil Nadu politics is fully dominated by the ethnic and regional political parties interested in playing national role in the federal polity and thus Tamil Nadu is in the mainstream more than the National Political Parties.

Conclusion

The ethnic political parties in the process of competing with each other to capture power forged an alliance with any one of the national political parties. By making political alliances with parties to maximise the electoral prospects, cadres have been oriented to see the output aspect of the political process instead of seeing the means aspect of the polity. To safeguard the interest of the party and its leaders any value of the party could be sacrificed. There is no difference between the DMK and the AIADMK in forging alliance with national political parties. Objectives of the two parties, the DMK and the AIADMK, for making political alliances to contest the election are one and the same. The only difference is the context and not the content. The two parties have been helpful to the national political parties to establish roots in Tamil province. Expectations of the parties are the same. Outcome of the process will not be the same as the context differs.

Notes and References

1. Myron Weiner, *The Indian Paradox: Essays in Indian Politics*, New Delhi: Sage Publications, 1989, p. 21.
2. Arend Lijphart, *The Puzzle of Indian Democracy: A Reinterpretation*, New Delhi: Rajiv Gandhi Institute of Contemporary Studies, 1994 (RGICS Paper No. 18), p.1.

3. Sudipta Kaviraj, *Politics in India*,Delhi: Oxford University Press, 1997, pp. 1-35.
4. Robert L. Hardgrave Jr., *Dravidian Movement*, Bombay: Popular Prakashan, 1965.
5. G.Palanithurai, "Tamil Nationalism as a factor in Indian Politics", *The Indian Journal of Political Science*, Vol. 43, No.3, (July 1982-Dec. 1984).
6. Many frameworks have been developed over the years to explain ethnicity and ethnic group relationship. Frameworks and approaches have been classified by Urmila Phadnis in her work. All the approaches have been used by native scholars to study Tamil ethnicity. For more details see Urmila Phadnis, *Ethnicity and Nation-Building in South Asia*, New Delhi: Sage Publications, 1989.
7. T.V. Sathyamurty, "Political Change in Tamil Nadu", *Review of Development and Change*, Vol. II, No. I, (Jan-Jun, 1997), p. 7.
8. Marguerite Ross Barnett, *Politics of Cultural Nationalism in South India*, Princeton: Princeton University Press, 1970.
9. Marxist generally viewed it as an epiphenomenon.
10. Morris-Jones, *Government and Politics of India*, London: Hutchinson & Co. Publishers, 1967.
11. Myron Weiner (ed.), *State Politics in India*, Princeton:Princeton University Press, 1968.
12. Iqbal Narain (ed.), *State Politics in India*, Meerut: Meenakshi Prakashan, 1965.
13. Extensively Literature has been developed by the native scholars. For more details, see G. Palanithurai, "A General Framework for the Analysis of State Politics", in *Caste, Politics and Society in Tamil Nadu* (Ed), G. Palanithurai, New Delhi: Kanishka Publications, 1994, pp. 1-7.
14. N. Ram "Dravidian Movement in its Pre-Independence Phases", *Economic and Political Weekly*, Annual XIV : 7 & 8 (1979).
15. G. Palanithurai, "Dravidian Movement: A Study in Reformulation" in *Ethnic Movement in India: Theory and Practice*, (eds), G. Palanithurai and R. Thandavan, New Delhi, Kanishka Publication, 1993, pp. 227-32.
16. G. Palanithurai, (Ed.), *Ethnic Movement in Transition: Change in Ideology and Culture*, New Delhi: Kanishka Publications, 1998.
17. M.S.S. Pandian, *The Image Trap*, New Delhi: Sage Publications, 1992.
18. C.A. Perumal and V.K. Padmanabhan, "Political Alliances in Tamil Nadu", *The Indian Journal of Political Science*, Vol. XLVIII, No. 4 (Oct-Dec, 1987), pp. 618-29.

19. G. Palanithurai, *Perceptions of Grassroots Democracy and Political Performance*, New Delhi: MD Publications, 1998.
20. K. Sivathambi, *The Tamil Film as a Medium of Political Communication*, Madras: New Century Book House, 1981.
21. R. Thandavan, *All India Anna Dravida Munnetra Kazhagam*, Madras: Tamil Nadu Academy of Political Science, 1987.
22. G. Palanithurai, "Ethnic Political Parties and Electoral Behaviour in Tamil Nadu" in *Ethnic Movement in India: Theory and Practice*, (Eds.), G. Palanithurai and R. Thandavan, New Delhi: Kanishka Publications, 1993. pp. 157-78.
23. *Ibid.*
24. G. Palanithurai, *Indian Polity : Myth and Reality*, New Delhi: Kanishka Publication, 1994.
25. The middle class has achieved its goal and it is believed that the Dravidian Movement is organised by the backward class. For more details see S. Saraswathi, *Minorities in Madras State*, Delhi: Impel India, 1974 and Indhu Rajagopal, *The Tyranny of Caste: The Non-Brahmin Movement and Political Development in South India*, New Delhi: Vikas Publishing House, 1985.

Bibliography

Abraham, M.F., *The Agony of India.* Madras : East-West Publishers, 1998.

Almond, G.A. and Coleman, *J.S., Politics of the Developing Areas.* Princeton: Princeton University Press, 1960.

Banerjee, A.M. and Chandrasekaran, K.A., (eds.). *Renewing Governance: Issues and Options.* New Delhi: Tata McGraw Hill Publishing Company Limited, 1996.

Bardhan, Pranab, "The state against society: The great divide in Indian Social Science Discourse" in *Nationalism, Democracy and Development,* (eds.) Sugata Bose and Ayeshah Jalal. Delhi: Oxford University Press, 1977.

Barnett, M.R., *Politics of Cultural Nationalism in South India.* Princeton: Princeton University Press, 1970.

Berelson, Bernard. "Democratic Theory and Public Opinion" in *Political Behaviour: A Reader in Theory and Research,* (eds.) Eulau Heinz, Eldersveld S.J. and Janowitz Morris. New Delhi: Amerind Publishing Co. Pvt. Ltd., 1972.

Bose, Arun. *India's Social Crisis.* Delhi: Oxford University Press, 1985.

Bread for the World Institute. *Hunger 1994: Transforming the Politics of Hunger.* MD USA: Bread for the World Institute, 1993.

Cernea, M.M. (ed.). *Putting People First: Sociological Variables in Rural Development Project.* New York: Oxford University Press, 1985.

Chelliah, R.J. *Towards Sustainable Growth: Essays in Fiscal and Financial Sector Reforms in India.* Delhi: Oxford University Press, 1996.

Chopra, K. Kadekodi, G.K. and Murthy, M.N. *Participatory Development: People and Common Property Resources.* New Delhi: Sage Publications, 1990.

Dahl Signel Lise. *Sustainable Livelihood Security: Case Study in Sivaranthakam Village.* Working Paper. Madras: MSSRF, 1995.

Department of Political Science and Development Administration. *From Participation to Self Governance.* Gandhigram: Gandhigram Rural Institute, 1998.

Department of Rural Development. *Responsibilities and Powers Handed over to Panchayats*. Chennai: Government of Tamil Nadu, 1998.

DMK, *Manifesto of Dravida Munnetra Kazhagam*. Chennai: Party Publication, 1996.

Dube, S.C., *Understanding Change: Anthropological and Sociological Perspective*. New Delhi: Vikas Publishing House, 1992.

Easton, David, *The Political System*. New York: Wilev and Sons, 1953.

Easton, David, *A Framework for Political Analysis*. Englewood Cliff, N.J.: Prentice Hall, 1965. .

Easton, David, *A System Analysis of Political Life*. New York: Wiley and Sons, 1965.

Elazer, D.J., "Opening the Third Century of American Federalism: Issues and Prospects", *The Annals of the American Academy of Political and Social Science* (May, 1990).

Esman, M.J., "The maturing of development Administration", *Public Administration and Development*. 8:2 (1988).

Gandhi, M.K., *Village Swaraj*. Ahmedabad: Navajeevan Publishing House, 1962.

Ghosh, Jayati., "Development strategy in India: A Political Economy perspective" in *Nationalism, Democracy and Development: State and Politics in India*, (eds.) Sugata Bose and Ayesha Jalal. Delhi: Oxford University Press, 1998.

Government of Tamil Nadu, *Tamil Nadu Local Bodies Act, 1994*. Chennai: Publication Division, 1995.

Gupta, Dipankar, "Continuous Hierarchies and Discrete Castes", *Social Stratification*, (ed.) Dipankar Gupta. Delhi: Oxford University Press, 1997.

Gulati, Ashok, "Changing Gears", *Seminar*. 433 (September, 1995).

Hangen, Welles. *After Nehru Who?* London: Pupert Hart Davis, 1963.

Hardgrave, Robert L., *Dravidian Movement*. Bombay: Popular Prakashan, 1965.

Hàrrison, Slig S., *India: The Most Dangerous Decades*. Princeton: Princeton University Press, 1960.

Hasan, Zoya, Jha, S.N. and Khan, Rasheeduddin (eds.), *The State Political Process and Identity: Reflections on Modern India*. New Delhi: Sage Publications, 1989.

INCPF. *Uncommon Opportunities: An Agenda for Peace and Equitable Development*. London: Zed Books, 1994.

INCPF, *Developing Human Resourcefulness: Strategies to Eradicate Poverty in the 1990's*. California: INCPF, 1995.

Indira Gandhi Memorial Trust. *Redefining the Good Society*. New Delhi: Wiley Eastern Limited, 1995.

Jacobs, Garry, Krishnamorthy, N. and Ramakrishnan. N., *Kamadhenu*. Madras: Southern Publications, 1988.

Jacobs, Garry, *Development Education: An Introductory Explanation*. Pondicherry: The Mothers Service Society, 1982.

Javeed Alam, "Political articulation of mass consciousness in present day India" in Zoya Hasan, S.N. Jha and Rasheeduddin Khan (eds.), *The State Political Process and Identity: Reflections on Modern India*. New Delhi: Sage Publications, 1989.

Jayaram and Saberwal Satish (eds.), *Social Conflict*. Delhi: Oxford University Press, 1996.

Jha, P.S, "The five years of Narasimha Rao", *The Hindu*. (7.4.1996).

Jha, P.S, "Corruption and Nation Building", *The Hindu*. (4.9.1997).

Kaare Storm, "Party Goals and Government Performance in Parliamentary Democracies". *The American Political Science Review*. (1972).

Kaviraj, Sudipta, "On state, Society and discourse in India" in *Rethinking Third World Politics*, (ed.), James Manor. London: Longman, 1991.

Kholi, Atul, *Democracy and Discontent: India's Growing Crisis of Governability*. Cambridge: Cambridge University Press, 1991.

Kholi, Atul. "Crisis of Governability" in *Politics in India*, (ed.) Sudipta Kaviraj. Delhi: Oxford University Press, 1997.

Kothari, Rajni. "Interpreting Indian Politics: A Personal Statement" in *Crisis and Change in Contemporary India*, (eds.), Upendra Baxi and Bikhu Parekh, New Delhi: Sage Publications, 1995.

Kothari, Rajni, *State Against Democracy*. Delhi: Ajanta Publications, 1988.

Krishnakumar, Asha, "Eradicating Hunger: The quest for a food secure world", *Frontline* (November 15, 1996).

Kumarappa, J.C., *Economy of Permanence*. Varanasi: Sarva Seva Sangh Prakashan, 1962.

Lijphart, Arend, *The Puzzle of Indian Democracy: A Reinterpretation*. New Delhi: Rajiv Gandhi Institute for Contemporary Studies, 1994.

LRSA, *The Politics of Panchayati Raj*. Chengalpattu: Legal Resources for Social Action, 1990.

McCarthy, Paul, *Postmodern Desire Learning from India*. New Delhi: Dromilla & Co. Publishers, 1994.

Maheswari, S.R., *Rural Development in India*. New Delhi: Sage Publications, 1985.

Maheswari, S.R., "Constituency Linkage of National Legislators in India", *Legislative Studies Quarterly* (Aug., 1976).

Manor, James (ed.). *Rethinking Third World Politics*. London: Longman, 1991.

Mathew, George. *Panchayati Raj: From Legislation to Movement*, New Delhi: Concept Publishing Company, 1996.

Mathur, B.C., "Emerging Issues in Public Administration", *Indian Institute of Public Administration Souvenir* (1998).

Mathur, Hari Mohan, *Administering Development in the Third World: Constraints and Choices*. New Delhi: Sage Publications, 1986.

Meenakshi Sundaram, S.S., *Decentralization in Developing Countries*. New Delhi: Concept Publishing Company, 1994.

Merkl Peter, H., *Modern Comparative Politics*. Illinois: The Dryden Press, 1977.

Mezey Michael L., *Comparative Legislatures*. Durham: Duke University Press, 1979.

Mezey Michael L., "The functions of Legislatures in the Third World", in *Handbook of Legislative Research*, (eds.) Gerhard Loewenberg, Samuel C. Patterson and Malcolm E. Jewell, Cambridge: Harvard University Press, 1985.

Mill J.S., *Considerations on Representative Government*, New York: Liberal Arts Press, 1958.

Ministry of Rural Areas and Employment. *Powers and Functions of Panchayat Raj Institutions: A Framework*, New Delhi: Ministry of Rural Areas and Employment, 1994.

Ministry of Rural Areas and Employment. *73rd Constitutional Amendment Act.*, New Delhi: Ministry of Rural Areas and Employment, 1993.

Ministry of Rural Areas and Employment. *Programmes for Change*. New Delhi: Ministry of Rural Areas and Employment, 1997.

Morris-Jones, *Government and Politics of India*, London: Hutchinson & Co. Publishers, 1967.

Narain, Iqbal, (ed.). *State Politics in India*, Meerut: Meenakshi Prakashan, 1965.

Narayanasamy, S., "Constructive programme towards the Twenty-First Century", *Gandhi Marg* (Oct.-Dec. 1997).

McNamara, Robert S., *Address to the Massachusetts Institute of Technology*. Cambridge: Massachusetts, 1977.

Oommen, T.K., "Changing paradigms of Development: The Evolving Participatory Society". *Journal of Social and Economic Development*. 1:1 (Jan.-June, 1998).

Palanithurai, G., "Tamil Nationalism as a factor in Indian Politics", *The Indian Journal of Political Science*. 43:3 (July 1982-Dec. 1984).

Palanithurai, G., *Indian Polity: Myth and Reality*. New Delhi: Kanishka Publishers and Distributors, 1989.

Palanithurai, G., *The Role Perception of Legislators: A Case Study of Tamil Nadu*, New Delhi: Konark Publications, 1991.

Palanithurai, G. and Thandavan, R. (eds.), *Perspectives on Indian Regionalism.* New Delhi: Kanishka Publishers and Distributors, 1992.

Palanithurai, G., *Polyethnicity in India and Canada*, New Delhi: MD Publications, 1997.

Palanithurai, G., "Dravidian Movement: A Study in Reformulation" in *Ethnic Movement in India: Theory and Practice*, (eds.), Palanithurai, G. and Thandavan, R. New Delhi: Kanishka Publications, 1993.

Palanithurai. G. and Thandavan, R. (eds.), *Ethnic Movement in Transition: Change in Ideology and Culture*, New Delhi: Kanishka Publications, 1993.

Palanithurai, G., "Ethnic Political Parties and Electoral Behaviour in Tamil Nadu" in *Ethnic Movement in India: Theory and Practice*, (eds.), Palanithurai, G. and Thandavan, R., New Delhi: Kanishka Publications, 1993.

Palanithurai, G., "General Framework for the Analysis of State Politics" in *Caste Politics and Society in Tamil Nadu*, (ed.), Palanithurai, G., New Delhi: Kanishka Publishers, 1994.

Palanithurai, G., *People's Perception of Politics: An Indian Perspective.* New Delhi: Kanishka Publishers and Distributors, 1995.

Palanithurai, G., *Perception of Grassroots Democracy and Political Performance*, New Delhi: MD Publications, 1995.

Palanithurai, G., (ed.). *Empowering People: Issues and Solutions.* New Delhi: Kanishka Publishers and Distributors, 1997.

Palanithurai, G., *Have our hopes belied?* Gandhigram: Rajiv Gandhi Chair for Panchayati Raj Studies, 1997.

Palanithurai, G., *Report of the Training Programme for Gram Panchayati Presidents of Dindigul and Sivagangai District.* Gandhigram: Rajiv Gandhi Chiar, 1998.

Palanithurai, G., *Containing Corruption at the Micro Level: An Experiment.* Gandhigram: Rajiv Gandhi Chair, 1998.

Palanithurai, G., *Empowering People for Prosperity*, New Delhi: Kanishka Publications, 1994.

Palanithurai, G., *New Panchayati Raj System at Work: An Evaluation.* New Delhi: Concept Publishing Company, 1999.

Pandian, M.S.S., *The Image Trap*, New Delhi: Sage Publications, 1992.

Parekh, Bhikhu, "Jawaharlal Nehru and the Crisis of Modernization" in *Crisis and Change in Contemporary India* (eds.), Upendra Baxi and Bhikhu Parekh. New Delhi: Sage Publications, 1995.

Patel, A.J., "The Doctrine of Swaraj in Gandhi's Philosophy" in *Crisis and Change in Contemporary India*, (eds.), Upendra Baxi and Bhikhu Parekh, New Delhi: Sage Publications, 1995.

Paul, Hartmann, Patil, B.R. and Dighe, Anith, *The Mass Media and Village Life: An Indian Study*. New Delhi: Sage Publications, 1989.

Perumal, C.A. and Padmanabhan, V.K., "Political Alliances in Tamil Nadu", *The Indian Journal of Political Science*. XLVIII: 4 (Oct.-Dec., 1987).

Phadnis, Urmila. *Ethnicity and Nation Building in South Asia*. New Delhi: Sage Publications, 1989.

Population Foundation of India, *State of India's Population*. New Delhi: PFI Publication, 1998.

Pye, L.W. "Identity and the Political Culture" in Leonard Binder *et al. Crises and Sequences in Political Development*. Princeton: Princeton University Press, 1971.

Pye, L.W. *Aspects of Political Development*, New Delhi: Amerind Publishing Co. Pvt. Ltd., 1972.

Rajagopal, Indhu, *The Tyranny of Caste: The Non-Brahmin Movement and Political Development in South India*. New Delhi: Vikas Publishing House, 1985.

Rajiv Gandhi Foundation, *Group Report of Colloquia on Decentralised Governance, Political Economy and Administration (Southern State)*. New Delhi: RGF, 1998.

Rajiv Gandhi Foundation, *Proceedings of National Workshop on Panchayati Raj*, New Delhi: RGF, 1993.

Rajiv Gandhi Foundation, *Revitalization of Panchayati Raj in India*, New Delhi: RGF, 1997.

Ram, N., "Dravidian Movement in the pre-Independence Phases", *Economic and Political Weekly*, Annual XIV: 798 (1979).

Roy, Ramashray and Srivastava, R.K., *Dialogues on Development: The Individual Society and Political Order*, New Delhi: Sage Publications, 1986.

Saberwal, Satish, *India: The Roots of Crisis*, Delhi: Oxford University Press, 1986.

Saraswathi, S., *Minorities in Madras State*, Delhi: Impel India, 1974.

Sathyamoorthy, T.V., "Political change in Tamil Nadu", *Review of Development and Change*, 11:1 (Jan.-June, 1997).

Sen, Amartya. "How India has fared?", *Frontline* (Aug. 1997).

Seth, D.L., "Social Basis of Political Crisis", *Seminar* (Jan. 1982).

Singh, S.S., Mishra, Suresh and Pratap, Sanjay. *Legislative Status of Panchayati Raj in India*, New Delhi: Indian Institute of Public Administration, 1997.

Sivard, Ruth Leger, *World Military and Social Expenditure 1991*, Washington, D.C.: World Priorities, 1991.

Siva, Vandana, "The Problem", *Seminar*, 433 (September, 1995).

Sivathambi, K., *The Tamil Film as a Medium of Political Communication*, Madras: New Century Book House, 1981.

State Planning Commission, *Interim Report on the Entrustment of Powers to Panchayats*, Chennai: State Planning Commission, 1997.

State Planning Commission, *Report on the Entrustment of Powers to Panchayats*, Chennai: State Planning Commission, 1997.

Subramanian, C., "An Agenda of Action I & II", *The Hindu* (18-7-1997).

Swaminathan, M.S. and Nair, K.N.N.S., *New Paradigm of Agricultural Research for Sustainable Food Security in the Asia-Pacific Region*. Chennai: M.S. Swaminathan Research Foundation, 1994.

Swaminathan, M.S., "Pathway to Rural Prosperity", *The Hindu: Survey of Indian Agriculture 1997*. Madras: The Hindu Publications, 1997.

Swaminathan, M.S., Rajagopal, S. and Sharada, S., *Hunger Free Area Programme*. Working Paper, Chennai: MSSRF, 1996.

Thandavan R. *All India Anna Dravida Munnetra Kazhagam*, Madras: Tamil Nadu Academy of Political Science, 1987.

Tharyan P., *India: The Critical Decade After Nehru*, New Delhi: Sterling Publishers, 1974.

UNDP, *Human Development Report 1997*, New Delhi: Oxford University Press, 1977.

UNDP and MSSRF, *Agenda for a Food Secure Asia-Pacific Region by 2010 AD*. Chennai: M.S. Swaminathan Research Foundation, 1994.

Weiner, Myron, *The Indian Paradox*, New Delhi: Sage Publications, 1989.

Weiner, Myron (ed.), *State Politics in India*, Princeton: Princeton University Press, 1968.

Yadav, Yogendra, "Indian Democracy I & II", *The Hindu* (18, 19-8-1997).

Index